GREAT LIES

GREAT LIES

Jo Donnelly

ANGUS
& ROBERTSON
PUBLISHERS

AN ANGUS & ROBERTSON BOOK

Angus & Robertson (UK)
16 Golden Square, London W1R 4BN,
United Kingdom, and
Collins/Angus & Robertson
Publishers Australia
Unit 4, Eden Park, 31 Waterloo Road,
North Ryde, NSW, Australia 2113
William Collins Publishers Ltd
31 View Road, Glenfield, Auckland 10,
New Zealand

First published in the United Kingdom by
Angus & Robertson (UK) in 1990.
First published in Australia by
Collins/Angus & Robertson Publishers in 1991.

Text copyright © Jo Donnelly 1990
Illustrations copyright © Frank Rodgers 1990

Typeset in Great Britain by New Faces, Bedford

Printed in Finland

British Library Cataloguing in Publication Data

Donnelly, Jo
 Great lies : the ultimate fibbers handbook.
 I. Title
828. 9409

ISBN 0 207 16877 6

For Chiqui,
a constant course of inspiration

Contents

Introduction

Nobody approves of lying. God is against it. The government is against it. Church leaders are against it. Big business is against it. Lying was the one thing that always made your mother's jaw set in that peculiar way and her eyes grow cold. In fact, no sooner did you learn to speak than your mother was giving you lectures about always telling the truth. 'It's a sin to tell a lie,' she told you. 'Honesty is the best policy.' 'You can trust a thief, but never a liar.' You nodded your little head wisely. This isn't such a bad planet to have been born on, you thought to yourself. Chocolate biscuits and honest inhabitants. A person can feel safe here, you thought to your young self. Secure. Trusting. Your mother then went on to tell you about what happened to the boy who cried 'Wolf!' 'Tut tut tut,' you said, 'what did he expect?' She told you about Pinnochio and his nasal problems. You smiled at your mother. 'Serves him right,' you said. Your mother gave you a hug.

'Mother,' you said, carried away by your mother's enthusiasm, 'who are some of the famous people who never lied? Anybody we know?' Your mother's kindly, loving face grew thoughtful as she tried to think of some historical figures whom she could present to you as role models. Her mind jogged back through the centuries. How about the kings and queens? How about all those important political leaders? How about the great composers, writers and artists? Explorers? Hostesses? Inventors? Missionaries? Shop-keepers? Can-can dancers? That frown line appeared on the bridge of your mother's nose. Oddly enough, people of inspirational honesty seemed to be a little thin on the ground in the general history of Western civilization. She concentrated for a few minutes on the twentieth century. A little tricky, the twentieth century, thought your mother. The only person who always told the truth about what he was doing was Hitler. 'Well,' she said at last, 'there is Mother Teresa.' You happily accepted the chocolate biscuit she offered you. Oh, come on, she silently chided herself, we're talking about a few thousand years here. There must be *somebody* else. The frown line grew deeper. 'I've got it!' she cried excitedly – and so unexpectedly that the biscuit leapt out of your tiny hand. 'Jesus Christ.' You looked around nervously. 'But, Mother,' you stammered, 'I thought cursing was as bad as lying.' 'No, no,' said your mother impatiently. 'That was his name. Jesus. Jesus Christ. Now there was an honest man.' 'Oh,' you sighed, retrieving your snack from the floor your mother always claimed was so clean you could eat off it, 'Jesus Christ.' Your mother didn't go on to tell you what had happened to him. Instead she told you to throw your biscuit away and take another one: it had been on the floor.

But, in spite of your mother's advice, one of the more interesting aspects of human behaviour is the fact that though we all take the private and public stance that lying is a thing to be condemned, avoided and shunned, we all accept it as a natural, even inevitable, part of our daily lives. Everybody does it. Everybody expects to have it done to them. It is, in fact, so accepted that not only does it not cause the most upstanding of citizens to blink or blush, most of us don't even notice when it's happening.

For instance.

You go into the clinic for your holiday shots. You roll up your sleeve. You start chatting to the nurse about the weather in Brazil, a topic in which she seems extremely interested. She rubs a little antiseptic on your arm. She smiles. 'You're just going to feel a little pinch,' she says brightly. 'You're not worried, are you?' Do you say, 'Oh ho ho, I've heard that one before?' Do you say, 'Oh, isn't it wonderful what modern medicine can do. Just a little pinch'? Do you say, 'Get that elephant-gun away from me, of course I'm worried' or 'I've heard of three people who died from that injection'? No. What you say is, 'Of course I'm not worried, ha ha ha.' And then, without even thinking, you fix your eyes on the poster about third-degree burns on the opposite wall and brace yourself for the swift but searing jab of pain you know is coming next. The nurse, who was once bitten by a typhoid injectee who hadn't been worried either, hopes that if you do react it will be to faint. As soon as your heart starts beating again you wipe the tears out of your eyes and say, 'Well, that wasn't bad at all.' Unless you are my Uncle Lester. In which case you go for the hand that holds the needle.

For instance.

You bring the car into the service station because of the slightly unpleasant sound it makes when you turn corners sharply or go over twenty miles an hour. Jim, the mechanic with the sincere blue eyes and the photograph of his children nailed to the office wall, is sympathetic as you tell him this latest development in your auto's medical history. He peers under the bonnet. He pokes around with this and that. 'Turn over the engine,' he says. You turn the engine over. He looks thoughtful, reflective. He is a professional giving you a professional assessment. 'Umm,' he says. You scurry out of the car to stand beside him. 'Well?' you say. 'What's the verdict?' He shrugs in that professional way he has. 'Well,' he says, 'it's hard to tell at this stage exactly, of course, but I don't think it's too bad. I think we can keep the costs down on this one.' Do you say, 'What do you take me for, a fool? Do you think I was born yesterday or something? Every time you tell me that, it costs me at least £200!'? Do you say, 'That's terrific, Jim, thanks a lot. That means I can buy the kids warm coats for the winter after all.'? Uh uh. You smile in a friendly, pleasant way, say, 'Great, I really appreciate how helpful you always are,' and start doing some serious thinking about taking out a second mortgage and finding a new mechanic.

Every day – in every area of our lives – we make and take a thousand lies. Not vicious lies. Not harmful lies. Not lies that count. No, of course not. But great lies. It'll be ready in an hour. Your cheque is in the post. Fresh today. I'll just have one. I was about to call you. Nothing like this has ever happened before. Of course I've never loved anyone else. We pretend, with no effort and less guilt, that we don't lie through our teeth every minute of the day – and everyone else pretends that they don't either. But lying saves time and angst. It makes everybody happier than they would be if they always told or had to listen to the truth. After all, you don't really want to hear that you'll be lucky if you ever see your stereo again. Finding out that you're not going to get paid, at least for a few months, plays havoc with your stress levels. Why should you want to know that the last head of cabbage in the shop - needed urgently for the borscht you're making for the Prime Minister's dinner party – has been sitting under the cash register with the cat for the last two weeks? You're hardly going to make a public announcement that you're about to eat an entire family-size bag of crisps. Not likely. Nor is it likely that you're going to explain to the man about to buy your car that the door always falls off like that. You're certainly not about to tell your fiancé that you loved the man you dated all through university a lot more than you'll ever love him. Think of it like this: life is an incredibly complicated, intricate, fragile, sensitive and dodgy machine - not great, perhaps, but the only one we've got – and lies are the lubricant that keeps the whole thing from blowing up in our faces.

Great Lies.

The truth at last . . .

1
Lying on the Hearth

That discussion with your mother about young boys who cry 'Wolf!' too often and gullible puppets with Italian accents was probably the first time that you thought about the concept of truth versus the concept of untruth. Up until then it's more than possible that lying had never occurred to you. If you accidentally knocked one of the good tea-cups off the table, it would never have entered your mind to blame the dog. If your mother discovered that someone had been eating the crayons again, you didn't look all innocent and say, 'It must've been Dad.'

'Who wiped their chocolatey hands all over the sofa?' your mother would shout.

Your eyes would grow to the size of ping-pong balls and you'd say, the truth as natural to you as wetting your nappies, 'Me.'

The other thing that wouldn't have occurred to you up until this fateful conversation was that anyone else would lie to you. When you were told that your face was going to freeze like that if you didn't watch out, you started checking the mirror three times a day. When you were informed that the Night Monster was going to get you if you didn't go to sleep immediately, you snuggled on down, immovable until dawn. Santa Claus sounded perfectly plausible. So did the news that bread crusts made your hair curly and carrots were good for your eyes. You had no trouble swallowing that story about being put up for adoption if you didn't put your toys away.

But after you and your parent had that nice chat about Mother Teresa, you went back to your room and you started thinking. Why is she telling me all this? Is this just an abstract, theoretical conversation, like the one about whether or not the tree makes any noise as it falls to the forest floor if there is no one there to hear it? Or is there more to it than that? Are there greater implications here than immediately meet the eye? You lay awake, long into the night, your little brain engaging in one of its first truly cosmic grapplings. It came as a shock, but out there, you decided, out in that big, hostile world filled with strangers, there must be people who would tell you untruths. People to whom you might even be tempted to fib yourself. But they were all out there, of course, on the other side of the garden gate. This was a comforting thought. At least there was one place on this globe where a person would always be treated with total honesty. Where black was black and white was white and you always knew where you stood. but then another, less comforting, thought entered your brain. You suddenly remembered being refused a second piece of apple pie at supper the other night because it would upset your tummy. You, a child who had eaten dog biscuits, crayons and sand without so much as a hiccup. A nasty suspicion joined the general grappling. Could it be? you wondered. No, nooo . . . That was too much. Not one's own family. Mother? Father? Big sister? Dear old Gran . . .? And then happened one of those fortuitous events, like the apple landing on Newton, on which turn the fate of mankind. A storm began. You went to the window and stared at the downpour. There was a rumble of thunder. The sky went white with lightning. Your parents had often assured you that rain was the angels crying; thunder was them playing bowls; and lightning was them shining their torches down on the earth. Some torch, you thought to yourself as the old chestnut tree at the back of the house suddenly split in two. More like a bleedin' flame-thrower. You tip-toed over to the book shelf and dragged down the *Encyclopaedia Britannica*, a book that had never been known to lie. You looked under 'Weather'. The *Encyclopaedia Britannica* it turned out, disagreed with your parents about the relationship between angelic activity and thunderstorms. You turned back towards the sky as another fork of lightning cut through the night. You resolved to have a little talk with your mother about the stork.

Things had begun to fall into place.

Lies your mother told you, part 1

You wouldn't like it.
You'll be too tired.
It's past your bedtime.
It's not going to hurt you.
There's nothing to be afraid of.
The shop ran out.
Next time.
We'll see.
Because I'm your mother.
The stork.
Aunt Susan doesn't have a television.

The lie your mother told you when you came home from your first day at school in tears because the minute you sat down at your desk every other child in the class started imitating an elephant

Of course your nose isn't too big. Whoever told you a ridiculous thing like that?

The follow-up lie your mother told you after the elephant incident

Sticks and stones may break your bones, but words will never hurt you.

What your mother told you when your team lost every game for two seasons running, when Mary Louise Weatherstone (as usual) was given the role of the Virgin Mary in the school play over you, when your poster for Dental Care Week was the only one not put up in the corridor, etc.

It isn't a matter of win or lose, it's how you play the game.

Lies your mother told you, part 2

Nothing going's to happen to you, Mummy's right here.
No one ever got anywhere by not telling the truth.
You're not really short.
You've got big bones.
It's only baby fat.
You'll grow out of it.
It's not what you look like that's important, it's what sort of person
  you are inside.
Because it'll give you nightmares.
Your face will freeze like that.
He's gone to hamster heaven.
Don't be ridiculous, no one's looking at you.
It's coming back into fashion.
Don't worry about me, I'm only your mother.

Lies your father told you, part 1

I'm busy right now.
Of course I wouldn't have
preferred a son.
Fighting never settled anything.
If it were up to me, I'd say fine,
go to the three-day rock
concert with the long-haired
guy on the Triumph with the
snake tattoo on his face. But
you know what your mother's
like.
Of course I'll understand.

I'm not going to lose my temper.
It isn't me I'm worried about.
It's your mother.
It has nothing to do with me.
You'll have to ask your
mother.
Because I'm your father.
We'll settle this fairly.
What chocolate egg?
I never said any such thing.
There's nothing to worry about.
The stork.

Lies both your parents told you

Because we're your parents.
We're not mad at you, we just want to know what happened.
We love all our children the same.
Some day you'll thank us for this.
We're only thinking of you.
This is going to hurt me even more than it hurts you.
Anything that began with: 'In my day . . .'
Anything that began with: 'When I was your age . . .'
Anything that began with: 'The other children never . . .'

We're sure you're going to like it.
In the future you'll remember this as the most important day of your life.
We'll decide this democratically.
We're all going to bed soon.
You can always tell us the truth.
You can talk to us about anything.
You'll be fine.
Of course we trust you.
It'll happen, you just have to wait.

The lie your parents told you the summer they sent you to Coventry to spend two weeks with your Aunt Lucy, a woman whose life was dedicated to cleaning and looking after her brother, Edward, the recluse who never spoke and who hated children, especially you

You're going to have a lot of fun.

The lies they told you when you phoned them after two days to beg them to come and take you back home, you'd do everything they asked you to do, they'd have no more trouble from you for as long as you lived

You can't come home now.
We'll come as soon as we can.
It'll get better.

Lies your father told you, part 2

It's not a question of money.
My door is always open.

When your father was going to take you fishing, camping, to Boulogne for the day

Next week/next month/next time/next year.

Lies your mother told you, part 3

I'll stay with you the whole time.
Just go one time to see how you like it.
I won't be long.
You're only allowed one ride on the carousel. The man wants you to get off.
Only this once.
I'll have that policeman arrest you . . .
You know I wouldn't interfere in your life . . .
It's your life.
I've given you every chance.
Your sister never behaved like this.
Your brother never gives me any trouble.
It's your own fault you're an only child.
Just lie down for a few minutes, you don't have to go to sleep.
Next time.
Later.
You'll spoil your appetite.
You're free to make up your own mind, of course . . .
You'll be sorry.
When you're older.
When the times comes.
Just in case.

The lie your mother told you when you were filling out the health form for work and wanted to know if there was any insanity in the family

No.

Or possibly

On your father's side.

Your father's great discipline lie

If you don't do what I say, I'm going to give your new bike to the boy next door.

The lies your mother told you when you were six years old and you found a blue box in that machine in the Ladies but she wouldn't let you see what was in it

Plasters.
Because you don't need one now.

You and your mother were going to visit her best friend, Aunt Mary, for the day. As you and your mother walked along, your tiny hand in her much bigger one, your little feet keeping step with her giant, purposeful strides, your mother chatting pleasantly about what a nice day it was and how pretty you looked and pointing out the interesting things you were passing – buses and lorries and cats sleeping on windowsills – you finally ventured to express some of your fears about what the afternoon had to offer. What if Aunt Mary made something for lunch that you didn't like? For instance, what if she'd forgotten what happened when you were forced to eat that grilled liver last time? What if she yelled at you again for doing something that wasn't your fault, like spilling your milk on the rug or treading on the cat? What if there was nothing to do? But what if there wasn't? What if nobody talked to you? What if she hadn't bought a television set yet? What if she forgot how you felt about discussing your hair cut? Your mother squeezed your tiny hand and turned sharply up the steps to Aunt Mary's house, a building that looked more like a mausoleum than a home, though you, of course, were too young to know about mausoleums. Your mother looked down at you with compassion, wisdom, affection and a smile that said, 'You're with me, you don't have to worry about a thing.' Your mother said

Don't be silly, darling, everything's going to be fine.

When lunch was being served, your mother turned to Aunt Mary and said

Oh, yes he eats anything.

When the cat scratched you and you spilled your tea on the sofa, your mother said

Stop crying, darling, Aunt Mary wasn't yelling at *you*.

As you boarded the bus back home, your mother said

There, now wasn't that nice?

Mealtime lies

You're going to love this.
I made it just the way you like it.
I can think of a lot of little boys and girls who would be grateful to have it.
For heaven's sake, it's not off.
Sour milk can't hurt you.
Just one little bite.
It doesn't taste like toads' eyes.
Bread crusts make your hair curly.
Carrots give you good eyesight.
Spinach makes you strong.
Cauliflower makes your skin glow.
If you don't eat everything on your plate millions of children in China [Europe, Africa, or Central or South America, depending on your mother's age and political astuteness] will starve [thus, not only lying to you about your responsibility for world hunger, but making you think that by eating your creamed onions you made everything all right].
Because your teeth will fall out.
Three little pieces of liver aren't going to make you sick.
It tastes better than it looks.
There is nothing in that soup that you don't like.
No one puts ketchup on cornflakes.
That's nothing.
It's not slimy.
Those slices are exactly the same size.
It's supposed to taste like that.
That's the way it's meant to look.
It tastes just like chocolate.
It's not bleeding.

Children's mealtime lies

I'm not hungry.
I'm full up.
I didn't eat anything before supper.
I don't like it.
Since now.
It smells funny.
It's the wrong colour.
I have to go to the toilet.

Mother notices that her small son has misgivings about the fried liver. She sees the way he shoves it under his mashed potatoes, the way he cuts it into itsy-bitsy pieces that he then moves around his plate in a restless manner. Nor has it escaped her notice that the dog is sitting very close to her small son. She exchanges a few words with Father about the incredible bargain she got today on two new pairs of shoes and when she looks back her small son has finished his meal. 'What happened to the liver?' asks Mother

I ate it.

The lies your mother told you when you wanted to know why Susan Hillman's mother's mashed potatoes didn't have lumps in them like hers

Because Susan Hillman's mother doesn't know how to make
   mashed potatoes.
Because the Hillmans are Methodists and they do things differently.

Lies your mother told you, part 4

Your father died at sea.
I never knew the whole story.
Other mother's children ring
   them every day.

It was just that your grandfather
   liked to travel.
Of course he was never in jail.
Big girls/boys don't cry.

Your father's sisters all had hair
   on their chests.
I wasn't being critical.
You know I don't want to do
   this . . .
I didn't tell a soul.
I love it.
Of course I was listening.
You were such a sweet baby.

I wasn't prying.
As soon as we get home.
It doesn't concern you.
I've got a headache.
You're too young.
You're too big.
That was the best nativity play
   I've ever seen.

Lies your parents told you about sex

If you really love each other.
It'll fall off.
You'll go blind.
But they don't enjoy it.
Just remember, honey, those
   people aren't really happy.
I have no idea.
No.
It's worth waiting for.
When the time comes.

The basic untruths brothers and sisters tell one another

Mum always liked me best.
Dad always said you . . .
You're adopted.
They made me.
It's your turn.
I'll do it for the rest of the
   week if you just do it tonight.
I promise.
Cross my heart and hope to die.

'Cause Dad said so.
I'm not going to lose it.
I'm not going to break it.
I'll pay you right back.
This time I'll let you win.
This time we'll play what you
   want.
Next time you can choose.
You started it.

More basic sibling lies

I won't forget this.
I'm not going to hurt it.
I'm not going to hurt you.
I'll put it right back.
It wasn't my fault.
It wasn't me.
I wouldn't touch your old dress [bottle collection, football, flute . . .] if it was the last one in the world.
I'm not going to forget.
I'll take care of it for you.
You're not going to miss just one.
I'd share with you.
It isn't ruined.
It was like that.
You weren't around to ask.
Tomorrow.

I did not cheat.
That's the way we play it at school.
Mum said I could.
How was I supposed to know it was yours/it was cracked/it would run/the wheel was going to fall off?
I'd tell you.
I'd do it for you.
You wouldn't want me to lie, would you?
I forgot.
I wouldn't want your old jumper anyway. It smells like a fish tank.
I was telling the truth.
They didn't have any.
I didn't think you'd mind.

THAT'S THE WAY WE PLAY IT AT SCHOOL.

The lie your sister told you the time you found her and her boyfriend locked in her bedroom while your parents were out

We were studying.

The lie *you* told your sister the time you found her and her boyfriend locked in her bedroom while your parents were out

I swear I won't tell.

The lie your Uncle Bob told your father when they went into business together

You can leave everything to me.

The lie your Aunt Lucy told your mother at their father's funeral

The last thing he said to me was that he wanted me to have the china and the good silver.

Your mother's return lie

That's what Mother said to me.

Aunt Lucy's reaction to this news

It must have been the medication.

Lies your mother told you, part 5

I just want you to be happy.
Some day your prince will come.
Boys are looking for a girl they
  can respect.
Nice girls don't.
Of course I didn't.
I don't remember.

Lies your mother told you, part 6

Glasses can be very attractive.
Of course I'm happy for you.
I don't want you to worry about
    me.
You didn't inherit those teeth
    from my side.
Do you know what happens to
    children who disobey their
    mother? They . . .

Lies parents tell waitresses, waiters and shop assistants

She's very sorry, aren't you honey?
They're usually so well behaved.
It's her birthday.
He's not mine. I'm minding him for a friend.

The lie your mother told you when you gave her the pen-holder made out of an old peach tin for Christmas

Just what I always wanted.

Why your mother was always the one who ate the black fruit gums/jelly beans/gum drops

She liked them.

Lies older siblings tell younger siblings

Just stand right here. I won't be
    long.
She didn't say I actually had to
    take you in with me.
There's not enough money for
    two.
Nobody's going to find out.
I've just had this brilliant idea.

It was your own fault.
It wouldn't have happened if
    you'd listened to me.
Nobody likes you.
She made me tell her.
It wasn't very good anyway.
It wasn't my idea . . .

Lies younger siblings tell older siblings

I didn't mean it.
It wasn't my fault.
Mum said you better not . . .
Not me.
I know what I'm doing.
It just slipped out.
Mum said I could.
Dad said I could.
You said I could.
I'm going to tell . . .
I'm not going to tell.
I didn't tell.
It was an accident.

The series of lies your sister told you when she realized how much better she'd look in your new red dress than you

It's a little tight in the bum, isn't it?
Are you putting on more weight?
I'm surprised you'd wear that shade with your colouring.
Is there something wrong with your breasts?
I just want to wear it to the party.
Of course I'll be careful.

The lie Marcia Clearwater told her little sister Mary when she sold Mary her old leather jacket for ten pounds more than she'd originally paid for it

Inflation.

The great sister lies

As close as two peas in a pod.
Sisters are supposed to share.
We have no secrets.
We're not just sisters, we're best
    friends too.
You're so much like mother, it's
    frightening.
That's not the way I remember
    it.
He told me he liked me better.
I'd never lie to you.
You think I'd do something like
    that to my own sister? Are
    you crazy?
That's just the way you acted
    when you were six.
I wanted to tell you, but . . .
I'll replace it, I swear.
I thought you didn't want it
    anyway.

Lies between brothers

Yes.
A couple of times.
Fantastic.
Because I know.
I just want one little bite.
Who do you think they'll believe?
That sound's not coming from next door.
I won't let anything happen to you.
I've done it a million times. I swear it.
I'll be right behind you.
Dad won't care.
I'll be right back.
They won't let you in.
You wouldn't enjoy it.
Then you're not really my brother.
You smell.
I think there's something wrong with it. Nobody else's looks like that.
They're never going to miss it.
Everybody does it.
It tastes just like chocolate.
They'll never know.
No reason.

Your mother said you could have that last slice of applesauce cake with walnut icing. You said. 'Oh, Mum, I really love you. Are you sure you don't want it yourself? I wouldn't want to eat it if I thought you were hungry.' Your mother said, 'I don't really care much for sweets.' You sat down at the kitchen table. Your fork was just hovering above the cake when your sister walked in. Your sister said your mother had promised her that slice of cake. 'Oh, darling, I'm really sorry,' said your mother. 'I completely forgot.' Your sister said your mother always did this to her, that you got everything and she got nothing. Your sister started crying. Not only did your mother always do this sort of thing to her, but she hadn't eaten for eighteen hours. You said, 'Oh, for God's sake, take the stupid cake if it means that much to you. I don't care.' Your sister said

I'm not hungry anymore.

You said

Well, neither am I.

Your mother said

There's only one way to settle this. I'll have to eat it.

The lie Marcia Clearwater told Mary to get her into the loft the time she and Nancy Ottinger locked Mary up in there for forty-five minutes

Just see if the light stays on when the door's shut. Then we'll let you out again.

General family lies

Grandma's just a little nervous, that's all.
Grandma's just a little hard of hearing.
Your father's had a hard day.
Your mother's got a headache.
No one remembers.

We know what's best.
It's you we're thinking of.
Who can you trust if you can't trust us?
Who else could you turn to?
Someday you'll understand.

The great family lie

Happy families.

The second greatest

Your family will never let you down.

The third

Nothing like this has ever happened in this family before.

The fourth

Father knows best.

The fifth

Who understands you better than your own flesh and blood?

The sixth

Safe in the bosom of one's family.

The seventh

Home sweet home.

Lies your mother told you, part 7

Of course I'd tell you if I thought they'd laugh at you.

You'll be sorry if you don't.

If it were up to me, of course, I wouldn't mind, but your father's not going to like this one little bit.

I'm sure there'll be a lot of children there.

Do what you please, it's your life.

I'm sure you know what you're doing.

I promise I won't be angry.

They didn't have chartreuse in your size.

I'd never try to tell you who to have as friends . . .

Just wait till you have children of your own . . . then you'll see what I've had to put up with.

I won't tell your father . . .

I won't tell your teacher . . .

I found it when I was straightening up your room . . .

Lies children tell their parents

Yes.
No.
I promise.
Of course not.
I didn't.
I did.
In a minute.
As soon as this show is over.
No reason.
I was going to do it.
You won't be sorry.
I looked everywhere,
I did look.
I heard you the first time.
Why me? It's always me.
You didn't say you had to cook it first.
I swear I'll look after it.
Every day.
It's not going to be like last time.
Okay, okay, I was just going to do it.
You always pick on me.
You blame me for everything.
It's not going to spoil my supper.
I fell asleep.
I did practise.
I will practise.
I can't practise.
I don't know how it happened.
Not me.
Everybody does it.

Everybody else has one.
It's not going to scare me.
I'm not going to have
   nightmares.
It's not going to make me sick.
I'll run away.
I really mean it.

Other lies children tell their parents

It slipped.
I was looking for something.
I thought you'd like it.
I only wanted to help.
I did it for you.
But I wasn't hungry then.
He hit me first.
I did hear something.

I didn't hear you.
Nobody else's parents make
   them . . .
None of my friends have to be
   home that early.
But you know where I'll be.
That was just that one time.
Well, it looked just like mine.

Your mother asked you what you did with all the junk that was on the floor of your room

I put it away.

You didn't stuff it under the bed, did you? asked your mother

No.

The interchangeable lies your father told your mother every time she asked him when he was going to fix the leak in the bathroom

Tomorrow.
Later.
I can't find my tools.
I thought you wanted this jar of
   pickles opened.
Just give me a chance to digest
   my dinner.

Right after this programme.
Well, why didn't you remind me?
It's too late to start it now.
I must've dozed off.
I'll do it when I get back.
Everything's always left to me.
What leak?

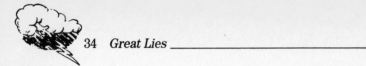

The lies your father told your mother when she, knee-deep in water and debris, suggested that perhaps a plumber should be called in after all

It's nothing.
I just have to make one little adjustment.
I know what I'm doing.
This is all your fault.
This is saving us a fortune.
You're going to thank me for this.

The lies husbands tell wives when the company holds the conference in Las Vegas

No one else is bringing his wife.
You wouldn't like it.
Do you think I'm going to be out enjoying myself? I'm going to be
    working my butt off the whole time.
The kids need you at home.

The lie your mother told you the day you realized you were the only child you knew who didn't receive a valentine

They were all probably lost in the post.

The lie your mother told you on the next St Valentine's Day

Of course it wasn't from me.

The lies your mother told you as you set off for your first day at school

It's what all the kids wear.
You're going to love it.
It'll be fun.
You'll make lots of friends.

The lies your mother told you when you returned, in tears, from your first day at school

They don't mean anything by it.
They're just jealous.
They'll stop if you ignore them.
They wish they had shoes like yours.

The lie Marcia Clearwater's mother told her the morning of the hurricane when they couldn't find Marcia's wellies and her mother made her wear plastic bags over her shoes

No one will notice.

A few of the lies husbands tell wives

It'll have to wait till the morning.
It'll have to wait till the spring.
You can't do it in this weather.
It's nothing, honey, don't worry about it.
I'll handle this.
I have to work late.

It wasn't expensive.
You know I could never look at another woman.
Of course I know what day this is.
It wasn't my fault.
I was listening.

A few more

I thought you'd thank me for
  giving your friend a lift home.
It'll come out.
One of the chaps at work.
I tried to get home in time.
Do you think I _enjoy_ travelling
  all over the world?
You should've let me handle it, I
  didn't want to upset you.
I don't think you've put on
  weight.
Did I say I'd take care of it?
  Then what are you worried
  about?

You've got no reason to be
jealous.
There's plenty of time.
I am under the speed limit.
Of course I'm not drunk.
You're the one who rides the
clutch.
You wouldn't understand.
It'll never happen again.
You could have come fishing
with me if you wanted.
How should I know?
I remember exactly.
What policeman?
I don't snore.
For heaven's sake, darling, I was
only kidding.

And more

It wasn't a criticism. All I said
was . . .
I'm not taking sides.
Of course I like your sister.
I don't know how you can say a
thing like that to me.
It was only a suggestion.
Nothing's going to go wrong.

It doesn't need a primer.
I did follow your instructions.
Sweetheart.
Don't mind me.
I'm happy if you're happy.
I was only thinking of you.
Everybody does it.

When the question is: Do you understand what I said?

Yes.

When the question is: You won't forget, will you?

No.

When the question is: I can trust you, can't I?

Yes.

Great marriage lies

Made in heaven.
Happily ever after.
Equal partners.
A marriage can't work unless both parties are totally honest with each other.
For better or worse.

Famous last marriage lies

You can tell me the truth.
I'd want to know if the situation were reversed.
Your father [mother] never knew.
We never had any secrets from each other.
I've never had one moment of regret.
You know you could never fool me.

I can always tell.
We never go to bed angry.
I love you just the way you are.
Of course I'm not trying to change you.
Fifty glorious years.
We never argue.
Still as in love as on the day we met.
We share everything.

Family lies about the car

I came out of the store, and what do I see but this dent in the bumper?
I wasn't the one who left the lights on.
Noise? No, I didn't notice any noise.
It's your turn to have it washed.

Family holiday lies

We never go where I want.
This year we're going to save some money.
You're going to have a good time.
There'll be plenty of children there your own age.

Family going-to-the-cinema lies

We're not going to be late.
There's plenty of parking.
The kids have promised to behave.
Next time you can choose.
Because it's too old for you.
Everyone brings their own popcorn.
It's not showing anymore.
I don't always fall asleep.
Really, Mum, it's not too violent.

Family activity (picnics, hiking, camping, renting a rowing-boat playing miniature golf, etc.) lies

We can all take turns.
Isn't this fun?

Family playing games like cards, Monopoly, Trivial Pursuit, Ludo or Sorry lies

It's only a game.
There's nothing to cry about.
I wasn't helping your sister.
I'm sure that answer's wrong.
I'm not upset.
I wasn't accusing you of cheating.

Your father came home from a hard day of gun battles and car chases and being tortured by international drug traffickers. 'Hi, honey! I'm home!' he called cheerfully as he walked through the door. 'Um um,' he said as he sniffed the domestic air. 'Is that fried chicken, mashed potatoes, creamed spinach and corn on the cob I smell?' Your mother, who had just come in from discussing the North Sea (or what's left of it) with the Prime Minister, said, 'No.' 'No?' repeated your father. All day, as the bullets flew and the brakes squealed, he'd been dreaming of fried chicken. With mashed potatoes, creamed spinach and corn on the cob. His heart was set on it. Even when he was dangling from the ledge of that building and the desperate international drug trafficker was stepping on his fingers the thought that had kept him hanging on was fried chicken. 'You can stick a slice of pizza in the microwave,' said your mother. Your father said

I'm not hungry anymore.
Oh, don't worry about me.
No, really, I don't want you to go to any trouble.
No, of course it doesn't matter.

A sampling of the lies that wives tell husbands

It was in the sale.
It wasn't really expensive if you think of how much use we'll get out of it.
It's nothing, dear, don't worry about it.

It wasn't my fault.
I don't know how.
I'll take it back if you really don't like it.
I don't think I can take it back.
I did exactly what you told me.

There's nothing wrong with my brother.

I'm not the only one who uses the phone, you know.

I'm not upset.

I didn't realize you were so attached to that smelly old thing.

I don't snore.

Of course I understand.

You know I would never tell anybody about your vasectomy/impotence/ premature ejaculation.

Especially not my sister.

I didn't say I wanted a baby.

They're a lot of fun once you get to know them.

I don't think they're going to be there.

It's Marcia Clearwater's.

Something came up at work.

I knew you wouldn't mind.

Nothing.

I was only reminding you.

It was just a question.

I must have dozed off.

A further sampling

Of course I didn't tell my mother.

You said you liked anchovies.

Of course I want to.

Harrison Ford's all right, but he's not as cute as you.

I like to see you enjoy yourself.

You know I'm easy to please.

I don't ask for much.

I'm happy if you're happy.

They didn't have it in green.

Everything's always left to me.

Nothing's going to go wrong.

It was already like that.

The sound of the car must have woken me up.

I wasn't sleeping.

I was asleep.

Of course I believe you.

It's not off.

Ten minutes.

Mother's great not-exactly a lie

We won't tell your father.

It's Mum's birthday. Dad is going to the family's favourite
take-away for a special celebration super. It takes two hours
for the family to go through the menu and agree about what
they want but at last the orders are all in. On his way to the
Golden Pagoda your father has an out-of-body experience and
a resultant loss of memory. When he returns with the food it
seems he's forgotten your mother's Hot Shredded Beef, her
favourite dish. 'Don't be ridiculous, of course I didn't do it on
purpose,' says Dad. 'She must have missed it out of the bag. If
you want I'll walk the three miles back and get it.' Your
mother says that of course she doesn't want him to do that.
'Look,' says Dad, 'I'm really sorry. But there's plenty of
everything else. Have some of the Shrimp Fried Rice or the
Chow Mein.' Your mother says

No thanks, I'm not really hungry.

The great all-purpose lie that covers every occasion, from
having the entire family forget your birthday to having to stay
at home and mind the sick baby on the night the Rolling
Stones invited you to a private party

Of course it doesn't matter.

The lie you told your little brother after he'd been standing
in the living room waiting for his lift to the Arsenal game for
forty-five minutes, practically berserk with anxiety and
excitement

They're here!

The lie your mother told you in the changing-room when you
started crying because those new summer shorts made you
look like the Michelin Man

It's the mirror.

If you didn't believe that, she said

It's the colour.
It's the material.
It's those shoes.
It's those socks.

Your mother was woken at three in the morning by something landing in the garden. Something in heavy boots. The dustbins crashed onto the concrete patio. The three Alsatians next door began barking for blood. She shook your father. Your father was having a really good dream, and, given the choice between staying in Tahiti and getting up to confront some intruder with a bad attitude, he wanted to stick to his dream. This is what your father said to your mother when she finally got him to open his eyes

I don't hear a thing.

Lies wives tell husbands when they want them to do something they don't very much want to do

It's okay, honey, I'll do it myself.
Bob next door said it wouldn't take him a minute.
I can always ask my sister to do it.
They especially asked for you.
I explained how busy you are.
Bunny Littletree's going to be there.
The drinks are free.
I had to tell them you'd do it.
It'll be fun.
You promised.
The other husbands will all be there.
Just do it this time and I'll never ask you again.

Lies mothers tell fathers to involve them more with their children

I know you're tired, darling, but I promised you'd take a look at it.
    You know how hopeless I am with anything mechanical.
All the other fathers are going.
If you don't do it they'll have to disband the troop.

If you could have seen her little face when I said you might not be
    able to coach the girls' football team.
I'm sure he didn't mean it.
There are some things only a father can do.
He's been looking forward to it so much . . .
You know they look up to you . . .
It's not going to kill you.
And whose fault do you think it will be if he ends up in jail?

Lies husbands tell wives when they want to get out of becoming more involved with the kids

I would if I could.
I can't.
Of course, I wouldn't miss it for the world, but . . .
It's not that I don't want to take thirteen six-year-olds to
    McDonald's . . .
Do you think they're not more important than my job?
Any night but tonight.
Next time.
Do you think I don't want to see the first year's version of *Aida*?
Of course I don't mind changing nappies. It's just that . . .
My father never did that.

Lies husbands tell wives when they want them to do something they don't much want to do

It's the last time I'll ask.
I'll make it up to you, I swear.
You're going to have a great time.
You don't have to do it if you don't want to . . .
I thought you wanted to go.
I distinctly remember you saying it sounded like a great idea.
Not long.
Just a few of the guys.

Lies parents tell children to get them to do things they would otherwise never do in a million years

The dentist is your friend.
You're going to have a ball.
There's nothing to be frightened of.
If you don't like it, we'll go right home.

Your brother never complained.
You'll sit right there until you eat every mouthful.
And afterwards we'll stop for ice cream.
Doesn't that sound good?

Lies mothers tell other mothers

She gets her looks from me.
All her teachers love her.
Oh, you can trust him with the cat.
She loves animals.
Animals usually love her.
She's never behaved like that before.
I'm sure he won't do it again.
Don't worry, she knows not to touch.
Well, I guess there's a first time for everything.
It wasn't really his fault.
You can't blame a little boy . . .
It's because she's so shy.
Boys will be boys.
She had a big lunch.
I really love this age, don't you?
Little angels.
I'm sure it's not contagious.
It must be all the excitement.

The lie Mrs Smith told Mrs Brown the day little Sammy Smith tried to knock little Teddy Brown's right eye out with a transformer

He must be over-tired.

Mrs Brown's return volley

The poor little thing.

Followed by Sammy saying

I'm sorry, Teddy.

And Teddy saying

Oh, that's all right.

At the end of the afternoon, Mrs Smith said to Mrs Brown

The boys get along so well. We must get together again soon.

Mrs Brown said

Oh, absolutely. I can hardly wait myself.

Lies your father told you, part 3

We'll discuss it later.
It's not a question of money.
I tried to get tickets, but it was
    sold out.
This will break your mother's
    heart.
I'll tell you when you're old
    enough to understand.
I did it for you.
You weren't around.
I'm not avoiding anything.
I'm not trying to influence you.
You'd try the patience of a saint.
I've bent over backwards to be
    fair to you.
I've worked like a slave for you.
You won't be punished if you
    tell me the truth.
I hear exactly what you're
    saying.

Father's great not-quite a lie

We won't mention this to your mother.

More lies children tell their parents

I never knew.
What biscuits?
I haven't seen them.
Maybe.
I don't remember.
I don't know.
I was only kidding.
See if I care.
Yeah, I really love it.
I thought I told you.
I wouldn't. Never.
I always look both ways.
I was just looking.
How did that get there?
But I didn't.
I never . . .
They're clean.
I only wore them once.
It was an accident.
I'll be right there.

The lie children tell their parents when the question is: Are you listening to me?

Yes.

When the question is: Do you understand what I said?

Yes.

When the question is: You won't forget, will you?

No.

When the question is: I can trust you, can't I?

Sure.

When the question is: You'll keep an eye on your little brother, won't you?

Yes.

And you won't make him cry, get him into trouble, or try to sell him?

Me?

You won't forget to bring him home with you, like last time?

I told you that wasn't my fault.

Three absolutely timeless children's lies

Nowhere.
Nobody.
Nothing.

One more

I changed them yesterday.

The lie you told your mother when she asked you if Marilyn Hatfield was jumping off a bridge if you would too

No.

Teenagers' lies

There won't be any boys or
  alcohol. Honest.
Of course you can trust me.
You never said that.
Her parents will be there the
  whole time.
I don't know anybody who
  smokes dope.

I don't know anyone who's ever
  had sex.
I'm going to the library to study.
  Alone.
I'm spending the night with
  Alice.
You can't call, the phone's been
  disconnected.

Everybody's wearing them
Nobody else has to.
You said . . .
I missed the bus.
No I didn't.
His mother's taking us.
I won't be long.
He's a really nice boy, you'd like him.

Just hanging around.
Someone must've stolen it.
I didn't know you were saving it for anything.
Yes, I'm telling you the truth.
You never wear it any more.
This is the last time, I swear.
It won't happen again.

What you told your mother when she found that packet of cigarettes

They're not mine.

What you told your mother when she found the packet of condoms

They're not mine.

What you told your mother when she noticed you were taking a pill every morning

They're vitamins.

Mother, Hoovering under the rugs in preparation for a visit by her own mother, comes upon a collection of magazines under the rug in the room of her teenage son. None of these magazines are concerned with music, motor mechanics, stereo systems, the contemporary theatre, or current events – unless you consider Miss April to be a current event (which, of course, some people do). When confronted with this considerable amount of evidence, her son says

They're not mine.
I don't know how they got there.
You mean you don't believe me?

Other teenagers' lies

I didn't do anything.
You never said I couldn't.
This boy at school lent it to me.
I found it.
I forgot.
I forget.
I left it at school.
I really appreciate this.
I didn't think you'd want to meet her.
You always over-react.
I was going to tell you.
I'm doing my homework.
I'm thinking.
We're going to study the whole time.
I figured you'd already be asleep.
I didn't want to wake you. I know how hard you work.
It's none of your business.

Hanging around.
There aren't any jobs.
I was only asking.
I was only thinking of you.
You won't regret this.
If only I'd known . . .
Me?
You must be joking.
I was just joking.
You never want me to have any fun.
I know what I'm doing.
I couldn't find a phone.
The line was busy.
I couldn't help it.
I don't know why you're asking me.
This time I'm going to stick with it.
I will try harder.

You are getting ready for your first date. You have been getting ready for approximately three days, but these have been the truly crucial five hours. You have extracted, as is appropriate to such an occasion, several solemn promises from your family. They will let you answer the door. They will say nothing to this boy that suggests that they have heard anything about him other than his name. They will lock your little brother in the cellar for as long as it takes your date to ring the bell, say hello to your parents, watch you put your coat on, and say goodbye to your parents. Your father will not ask this boy what his plans are after he finishes school, how his parents voted in the last election, or which his favourite football team is. Your mother will not try to feed him. Your sister will not laugh. No one will mention how many times you've changed your clothes since you got home from school. You are just brushing your hair for the last time when the doorbell rings. Your heart skips a beat. It's him! You hurry out of the bathroom, bumping into your sister who has been waiting a while to get in, and go calmly down the stairs. Just as you come in view of the front door, which, surprisingly, is open, you hear your mother say, 'Well, you must be Stephen. I'd recognize you anywhere. I'll just call her. She's been up in that bathroom all afternoon.' Several days later, when you're speaking to your family again, you ask your father why he had to bang on about Manchester United like that, why they let your little brother wake up the newts, why your mother made the poor boy eat that home-made cake that had been sitting in the pantry for the past two months, and why your sister was allowed to roam free. They look at you blankly. 'Can't you see how you embarrassed me?' you sob

We don't know what you're talking about.

Your father says

I was only trying to straighten him out.

Your mother says

It looked to me like he was enjoying himself.

You are fifteen. Your baby fat has not yet received the message that you've reached puberty, you haven't had a piece of chocolate or a plate of crisps for six weeks and still your face looks like the 'Before' advertisement for Clearasil. There are three girls at school who mug you every day for your dinner money and pretend to bark when you enter the classroom, and your English teacher, who hates you, always calls on you when she's sure you don't know the answer. 'You're one of the few people I've ever known who can sleep with her eyes open, Miss Clearwater,' your teacher says about once a week. The class always thinks this is funny. When you complain to your parents about your life and its problems they say

We wish we were fifteen again.

You don't understand, you wail. I'm living in teenage hell. Your father looks over his newspaper at you and says

You don't know when you've got it good.

Your mother, who by her own admission was never overweight, never had spots, and was always one of the most popular girls in her year, says

You're going through what everyone your age goes through.

Then your mother says

Some day you'll look back on this and laugh.

Your parents are going out for the evening, leaving your older brother in charge. Your older brother is a cretin. He makes you pay him protection money so he won't flush your goldfish down the loo. He's always borrowing your things without asking, and returning them – when he bothers to return them – broken. The last time your parents went out and left him in charge he had his friends over for a party and wouldn't let you come out of your room. Your parents (who suspect that something happened because the refrigerator had been cleared, but who don't know what because your brother

promised to drop spiders in your bed while you were sleeping
if you ever told) say to your brother, 'Now you'll take good
care of your little brother, won't you? No having your friends
over. No bullying him. That pizza in the freezer is for the both
of you. Right?' He says

Right.

'We mean it,' your parents say. 'If we think you took
advantage of your little brother you won't be allowed to go
out for the next three years. You understand?'

Mum . . .

'You promise?' says your mother

What do you think? You think I'd hurt my little brother? You think
I'd be mean to the best brother in the world? You think you can't
trust me?

To which your parents say

Of course not.

**Mother's teenager comes strolling through the door just as
Mother is giving the stew a stir. Mother glances out of the
window at the coal-black night. She looks at the clock. 'It's
late,' says Mother in a concerned, motherly way. 'Where've
you been ?' Mother's teenager reaches around her to remove
a bag of crisps and a box of biscuits from the cupboard and
says**

At school.

'Till seven at night?' asks Mother

Yeah.

**Mother's teenager is going out shopping. He needs a new
skull-and-crossbones bandana and a bat earring. While he's
out, though, he will probably pass other shops. Shops that sell**

things besides bondage trousers. Mother says to her teenager, 'Rocko, while you're out could you pick up a light bulb for the kitchen? I've got so much to do for the party tonight . . .' 'Sure,' says Rocko. 'Sixty watts,' says Mum. 'The screw-in kind.' 'Yeah, yeah I know,' says Rocko. 'You won't forget will you?' says Mother. Rocko says, 'Mummmm . . .' 'It's just that they don't sell them around here and –' 'Cool it, Mum,' says Rocko. 'I'm not a child, you know. I can buy a light bulb without having to have a note pinned to my jacket.' Mother apologizes. 'I know, I know,' she says, 'it's just that I've got all these people coming and if you forget –' 'Mum,' says Rocko, 'I'm not going to forget.' When Rocko returns, about ten minutes before the first guest arrives, Mother is there at the door to meet him. 'Thank God you're back,' she says, trying not to sound like a mother. 'What took you so long? I was worried.' Rocko, slightly stooped under the weight of all the bags he's carrying and with a new blonde streak in his hair, says, 'I don't know why you always worry. There's nothing to worry about. I just couldn't get a bus for hours.' 'Well, you're here now,' says Mother. She smiles brightly, hoping to encourage him to give up the light bulb. She knows that if she asks him directly he will accuse her of nagging, of not trusting him, of always being on his back. 'So,' she says, 'you did a lot of shopping.' Rocko says, 'Yeah.' 'What'd you get?' asks Mother. 'Stuff,' says Rocko, and starts heading for his room. She gives up. 'What about the light bulb?' calls Mother as he shuffles down the hall.

What light bulb?

Mother's teenager is going on a school field trip. Mother has packed enough sandwiches, pieces of cake, bags of crisps, carrot sticks and apples to feed a family of acrobats for a weekend. 'Mum,' says her teenager, 'what's all this food for? We're only going to the museum for the day.' 'You might, get hungry,' says Mother. 'Don't forget your umbrella,' says Mother. 'Umbrella?' squawks her teenager. 'The sun's shining It's practically a heat wave.' 'You never can tell,' says Mother. Mother's teenager, carrier bag full of food in one hand and umbrella in the other, staggers down the front path. Mother calls from the doorway, 'Wait a minute, love. You might need a sweater'

When asked if she is over-protective, Mother says

No.

The reason Mother's teenager never does anything for him/herself

S/he wouldn't want to spoil Mother's enjoyment.

Father and his small daughter are in the local mega-supermarket on a Friday night. His small daughter is doing the usual things that small children do in crowded supermarkets as big as airplane hangers at 7.15 on a Friday night. She keeps wandering off, tripping up other shoppers, putting things that are not on the list into the basket, singing Kylie Minogue songs at the top of her voice, hanging from the trolley, and playing hide-and-seek among the economy-size boxes of detergent. Father is beginning to understand why he has traditionally taken less of a role in child-rearing than Mother. Mother obviously has nerves of steel and is a sucker for punishment. It is as his small daughter knocks twelve boxes of chocolate cereal off the shelf that an announcement is made on the tannoy about a lost boy. Small daughter voices her concern for the lost boy. Father says

You know why that happened? It's because he was messing around, that's why that happened. That's what happens to children who mess around instead of behaving.

Small daughter, her eye on a pyramid of boxes of cereal that tastes like blueberries and sugar but is specially fortified with extra vitamins, says

I'm behaving.

Father looks sad and says

They haven't found him yet, you know.

Your mother is visiting you for the weekend. Despite the fact that you are a mature and independent adult with a good job and a lot of peer approval, the thought of spending a weekend with your mother has the same effect on you that the thought of having dinner with the Queen has on many other people. (Will you say something tactless about headscarves? Will someone mention modern architecture? Will she know your dress is hired?) You spend the week prior to her visit getting ready. No going to the cinema. No going out to dinner. No boogeying till dawn. 'You won't believe this,' you tell Harrison Ford when he asks you out on Wednesday, 'but much as I'd love to go white-water rafting, I've got to dust the lampshades. My mother's coming.' [He says, 'Of course I believe you.'] You fumigate your flat. You lug every portable piece of material – curtains and rugs and dishcloths, that sort of thing – to the drycleaners. You get down on your hands and knees behind the loo to make sure there isn't one smudge of gunge back there, you scrape the soap off the soap dish and the little clots of toothpaste from the toothbrush-holder. You spend Wednesday night, when you could have been clinging to Harrison Ford as the raft bounced over the rocks, dusting every lampshade in the house. Thursday night, Visit Eve, you sit up till 2 a.m. with a bottle of gin (the remains of which are destined to be hidden at the bottom of an economy-size box of sanitary napkins), making out a minute-by-minute itinerary for you and Mum. Friday morning, having telephoned the office to tell them you've caught that bug that's been going around, you are at the station to collect her an hour before she is due to arrive, just in case her train is early. The first thing you say as she gives you that first happy once-over of appraisal and a quick kiss on the cheek is

Mother! I'm so happy to see you!

Your mother is too tired to take a bus back to your flat. And though she appreciates that you've bought those nice chocolate croissants for breakfast that she made you walk four miles for last time she was here, she really feels she needs a little fibre this morning, so the cab has to make a quick stop outside the supermarket while you nip in for a

packet of muesli. 'I hope you haven't gone to any trouble,'
says your mother as the cab roars towards home. You say
Of course not, Mum.

You finally get Mum in the house, find the right sort of hanger
for her coat, put on the tea, and sit down for a nice mother to
daughter chat. Your mother, her eyes wandering towards the
corners of the ceiling in their endless quest for subversive
dust particles, says
How are you, dear?

You tell your mother how you are. You've had a new
promotion at work. You've started a course in furniture
restoring. Your friend, Sharla, the one your mother didn't like
because her eyes are too close together, has asked you to
walk across the Himalayas with her. You've bought a new
coffee-maker and you saw three very good films in the last
month. You do not tell your mother about your new interest
in white-water rafting or that you had three dates last week.
Your mother says
I never said I didn't like Sharla.

Then she says, 'So, any men in your life at the moment?' To
which you smile sweetly and say
Mother.
No.
I told you, mother, I'm happy as I am.

You have to run out to the shops because somehow you forgot
that your mother does not believe in low-fat milk, it makes
the tea a peculiar grey colour. When you come back your
mother is standing on a chair, checking out the shelf liner
(just changed, of course) in your cupboards (from which you
have evicted all empty spice packets and cereal boxes).
'Mother!' you shout. 'What are you doing, snooping through
my cupboards?' Your mother looks at you in that way she has
and says

You know I would never snoop through your things, darling, I was
looking for something.

_____

Later that evening, your mother emerges from her bath with half a bottle of gin in her hands. She would like to know what it was doing at the bottom of a box of sanitary napkins. You explain

Beats me.

Lies mothers tell their friends about their friends' children

Isn't she sweet?
What a little charmer.
I think his ears give him character.
It's not that I don't want you to bring Susie . . .
I'm sure there's nothing to worry about.
A lot of children don't start talking till three.
Really? I can't say I'd noticed.

I see what you mean.
Of course I'd love to hold her.
He just has a strong personality.
No, she's not bothering me.
I'm sure the teacher must be wrong.
She certainly is a talented little dancer, isn't she?
Oh I'd love to hear him play the cello.
You must be so proud.
Oh, I wouldn't worry if I were you . . .
They all do it.
He certainly has a lot of energy.

Lies sisters tell their friends about each other

She doesn't look so good without her make-up.
They're not real.
She's not really that pretty if you see her close up.
She killed my gerbil.
I had to do everything.
She's always been jealous of me.
Of course I love her, she's my sister.

I'm so happy she's done so well for herself.
I'm really the one who raised her.
Do you think she ever thanked me?
I did my best.
Looks aren't everything.
I'd rather be me.
She was ill at the time.

The lie your brother tells you when he wants to borrow more money, your mother tells you when she wants you and your sister to bury the hatchet, and your sister tells you when she pretends to forgive you for telling her husband exactly what you think of him

Blood is thicker than water.

The lie your mother told you when you were six years old and she took you out to eat at a Thai restaurant. After a meal that featured absolutely nothing a six-year-old child who did not come from Thailand would ever contemplate eating, she

ordered you ice cream for dessert. You looked down at your
dish as it was placed in front of you. 'Mum,' you said. 'Mum,
the ice cream's got sweetcorn on it.' Your mother said

Of course it hasn't.

**The reason you couldn't have a budgerigar, sit on a public
toilet seat, or share your ice lolly with the little boy next door**

You'll catch a disease.

**The reason you couldn't go to California with your parents,
ride your bike to your friend's house, go to the heavy metal
concert on your own, or call your best mate who'd moved to
Australia**

It's too far.

The reason you never had a birthday party

It's too close to Christmas.
Nobody's around in the summer

**The reason your parents wouldn't let you turn on the
television on a Saturday morning, leave your room until
they'd called you on Christmas Day, or practise your guitar**

It's too early.

**The reason your parents wouldn't let you watch the Saturday
night film on the television, go to that last-minute party, or
take karate lessons**

It's too late.

**The reason you couldn't come downstairs and have some of
the goodies when your parents had company, read for as long
as you liked at night, or finish beating your dad at chess**

It's past your bedtime.

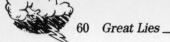

The reason you couldn't have an ice cream cone in December, go on a picnic on your birthday, or go camping with the other kids

It's too cold.

The reason there was nothing but cheese for supper, your party was cancelled, and your mother refused to help you practise football

It's too hot.

The reason you shouldn't scream your head off when your mother tried to wash your hair, the reason you weren't allowed to play your records at an audible volume, and the reason you weren't allowed to paint your room black

The neighbours will complain.

The reason you couldn't keep the cat you found, the box of chocolates you found, or the pair of socks someone at school traded you for your three-coloured pen

You don't know where it's been.

The reason your mother suddenly jumped up in the middle of supper and broke your record of 'The Shifting, Whispering Sands', the reason you came home from school and found the newt tank empty, the reason your best white shirt came back from the laundry tinged blue

I warned you.

The reason it was okay to do certain things

Everybody does . . .

And not others

Nobody does . . .

The reason you had to be nice to your grandmother, a woman who was always scolding you for something and who persisted in calling you by the dog's name

She's an old lady.

The reason you had to be nice to your grandfather, a person who never spoke to you unless he needed the peas passed

He's an old man.

The reason it was all right for your younger sister to run amok in your stamp collection, but not all right for you to slap her silly for it

She didn't mean it.

The reason your mother was never allowed to throw away the oil drum your father'd been keeping in the cellar for the past ten years, your sister's button collection, or the two hundred milk bottles you gathered from the dump

I might use it for something.

What parents tell their children after the stitches have been put in

That wasn't so bad, was it?

The great divorce lies

Amicable separation.
Mutual agreement.
Still good friends.
I'm glad he's found someone who makes him happy.
I'm not bitter.
No hard feelings.

The great Christmas lie. The one that occurs at about five-thirty-five on Christmas Day. It's the one that comes after the row about when to open the presents. After the children have stopped crying because they didn't get everything they asked for or Susie got something better than Angelina. After Grandma has been coaxed back into the sitting-room and Aunt Beryl has forgiven the crack about her cranberry sauce. After Mother locked herself in the bedroom for an hour because Father gave her another handbag and the children gave her a new tin-opener. After Uncle Albert passed out. After the vegetarians boycotted dinner. After the tree lights blew. After Dad started that argument about the Japanese. And after Ellen and her new boyfriend stormed out of the house because it's full of philistines who know nothing about art, music, or self-expression.

This was the best Christmas we've ever had.

The great family-gathering lies

It's always so nice to see everybody again.
I don't know why we don't do it more often.

The great hearth lie

A man's home is his castle.

[Although this is true in the sense that the homes of most men are draughty, don't have enough light, are constantly in need of repair, often have chickens, pigs, dogs and dwarfs underfoot, and are usually under persistent attack, it is not true in the sense that you are therefore entitled to spend other people's money, boss everybody around, or put the man next door in prison because he walked across your lawn. Nor is it true in the sense that in most cases it belongs not to you, but to the bank.]

2
Social Lies

With animals, it's usually a case of getting along with one another or not. You're either part of the group, not part of the group, a mate, or dinner. Grey areas in personal relationships don't exist. If one animal doesn't like another he will say so; not, perhaps, in so many words, but in a way that can't be misinterpreted – a gouging out of the eyes, a sharp fang in the neck, a quick slap around the head. Life is fairly simple when you've got four legs and a tail. You don't have to go to dinner with animals you don't like. You don't have to man the games stall at the church fete with Marcia Clearwater, pretending to be interested in her diet for three hours running. You don't have to give animals you loathe lifts into town.

But life, of course, is not that simple for us. You can't always avoid the people you don't like – sometimes you work with them, sometimes you get placed next to them at dinner, sometimes they're the only people at the party, sometimes you live together. You can't just walk up to a chap and punch him in the nose. You can't be rude to your bank manager. You can't refuse to go to dinner at your boss's house just because she's the most boring person in the world and her wallpaper makes you dizzy.

Alice through the Looking-Glass was not exactly the fantasy your teachers told you it was. Every day you step through your front door and into a world that is often not only hostile but relatively mad. Every day you have to deal with people you don't like very much, people you don't like at all, people who frighten or intimidate or dominate you, people who can make your life miserable or cost you your job, people you wish would just shut up and go away. This is why being able to socialize is such an important skill. And one that is taught to you almost as soon as you can hold up your head. First you learn not to push peas up your nose. And then you learn that life is lonely for the little boy or girl who hits anybody he or she doesn't happen to like.

To become a social creature is to learn how to lie with ease and grace. Only, of course, we don't call it lying. We call it being polite. We call it being diplomatic. We call it sparing others' feelings. We call it getting along with people. Being nice. Being pleasant. Being socialized.

Lies friends tell one another

I know exactly what you mean.
Nothing.
Would I lie to you?
What do you mean, mad at you?
I don't know what you're talking about.
Sure, I'll see you later.
I just don't feel like it.
You know I would if I could.
I didn't want to upset you.
I didn't mean it.
Of course it doesn't make you look fat.

They're coming back into fashion.
It was just a joke.
I appreciate how busy you are . . .
I've been phoning for days.
I wouldn't ask, but . . .
Oh, I understand.
Of course I understand.
It won't cost much.
It's not the money . . .
My lips are sealed.

Well, they didn't find out from me.

If you can't trust me, who can you trust?

There's nothing to forgive.

I know you're going to love it.

I'd forgotten all about it.

It's no trouble at all.

It was broken anyway.

So long as you promise you won't go to any trouble.

Delicious.

Great evening.

Oh, it was easy.

I hate to complain.

I have no secrets from you.

It's the thought that counts.

I'll be right over.

I never meant to imply that you were selfish.

All I was saying was . . .

You won't be sorry.

I insist.

It'll be much more fun if we go together.

It's Friday night. Everyone from the office goes to the pub. Time passes. Just as everyone is about to go home the one person who hasn't bought a round yet says

Whose round is it?

Further friends' lies

Of course I love it.

It's just what I wanted.

I don't blame you.

I think it makes you look very distinguished.

I never take sides.

Old? You don't look old.

Oh, do you owe me money?

You know how I hate to break a date . . .

I've got this stinking cold . . .

I'm not going to stay long . . .

I'm sure he's really nice once you get to know him.

No, I don't think you over-reacted.

In your position, I'd do the exact same thing.

I didn't want to hurt your feelings.

I knew you'd never forgive me if I didn't tell you.

I know it's not really any of my business . . .

I'll keep in touch.

I'll send you a card.

I'll phone.

The lies you and your friend tell each other when you meet at
the school reunion after twenty years. Neither of you are
seventeen any more, that's for sure. Twenty years of
mountain climbing have taken some of the peaches and cream
from your complexion. Twenty years of cooking in a pizza
restaurant have turned your friend from a lean machine into
the Michelin Man. The atmosphere is not the only thing to
have holes appearing in its upper surface. Both of you have
excellent opticians, though, so you spot one another from
across the crowded room. You rush into a warm embrace.
'Binky!' 'Bunny!' Smiling, you step back to take a good look
at one another. In almost one voice you both say

I'd have recognized you anywhere.

And then you both say

You haven't changed a bit!

You and your favourite market analyst, Bryan, are sitting
around the house one night, having a few drinks, discussing
the yen, when your very best friend in the whole world stops
by for a visit. She has never really met Bryan before, face to
face, but she has heard a lot about him. She knows that he is
absolutely passionate about Sam Peckinpah, that he can't
drink anything but twelve-year-old scotch, and that there is a
part of his anatomy that he refers to as Old Oil (because, he
jokes, it's always going up). She joins you for a drink. She
joins you for another drink. You are all getting on really well.
How nice, you think to yourself, to have your best friend and
the man you are thinking of committing yourself to serious
investments in get on so well. The night, as nights do, wears
on. It is time for your best friend to go. It is time for Bryan to
go (early meeting, has to do a little figure checking before he
turns in). You thought Bryan and Gulf Western were going to
be staying the night, but you do not, of course, mention this
to them. Instead you hug him and tell him not to work too
late. He says he'll try not to, but you know how it is. There is
a lot of kissing and goodbyeing at the door. A few days later
you get home from work to find your best friend on your

doorstep. **She has something she has to tell you. Going down together in the lift the other night, Bryan asked her for her telephone number. She didn't really want to, but, well she'd had a couple of drinks, and he was so insistent, and it wasn't like it meant anything or anything, so she gave it to him. He rang her as soon as he got home. He came over the next night, the night he told you he had to put together some figures for New York. Nothing happened. Of course nothing happened. She told him she certainly never wanted to see him again. But she had to tell you. 'You did?' you say. She says**

I knew you'd want to know.

As you pick up her coat and fling it into the hallway, trying very hard to fling her after it, she says

I don't understand why you're mad at me.

'You don't?' you scream. She says

No.

And then she says

I thought you'd appreciate my honesty.

Lies between people who aren't really friends, but pretend to be

It's always so nice to see you.
You're a sight for sore eyes.
Let's get together soon.
I'll ring you.
You know, I don't think I have your new address.
I'll be in touch.
I've been meaning to call you.
We were just talking about you the other day.
I can't tell you how many times I've picked up the telephone . . .
I'm telling you this for your own good.
I won't tell a soul.
I like to be honest . . .
You know I wouldn't be telling you this if I didn't care . . .

A favour? Anything. Just ask.
Don't thank me.
The pleasure was all mine.
It's really been fun.
Don't be such a stranger.
I hear what you're saying.
I hate to impose.
I wouldn't miss it for the world.
I'm really looking forward to going to the Japanese film festival
    with you.
You mean you were in the neighbourhood, and you didn't drop in?
Oh, I wish I'd known, I'd have loved to come.
Don't worry, I'll be there.

**You haven't spoken to X since the day he finally brought your
drill back after having it for a year. All of a sudden he's at
the front door. 'Boy!' you exclaim. 'What a nice surprise!'
After he's borrowed your drill, he says**

I'll give you a call next week and arrange to meet up.

To which you say
Great, I can't wait.

**You haven't spoken to A in about eighteen months. All of a
sudden she telephones you one Friday night and after asking
how you are, and how the parrot is, she asks you for someone
else's number. After you've given it to her she says**

I'll ring you next week and make a date to meet. Promise.

You say

Wonderful. I'll really look forward to that.

**You run into Y, whom you haven't seen in twenty-one months,
in the supermarket. By the frozen dinners. 'I never buy these,'
says Y, dropping the vegetarian curry she was holding into her
trolley, 'but I've been so busy lately, I have no time to cook.'
'Some of them are just as good as what you can make**

yourself,' say you. Finally someone else wants to get at the frozen dinners. 'It's been so good to see you,' says Y. 'It's been wonderful to see you,' say you. Then you say

I'll phone you next week and we'll get together.

Other lies between friends

Of course I want an honest answer.
Don't spare my feelings.
You know you can level with me.
I know I can level with you.
Nothing could ever destroy our friendship.
You know how shy I am.
You know how sensitive I am.
I know how sensitive you are.
You're generous to a fault.
You know you can count on me.
What do you really think?

More other lies between friends

You know I never say a mean word about anybody . . .
I was just thinking of you.
You mean you never got my message?
There must be something wrong with your phone.
I thought you said tomorrow night . . .
I was only trying to help.
I didn't think you'd want to know.
You'll thank me some day.
Anything.
Just tell me if I'm in your way.
I hope you'll tell me if there's anything I can do.

What's a few quid between friends?
I waited for hours.
I was stuck in traffic.
I thought it was over between the two of you.
I couldn't get to a phone.
The line was engaged.
That's funny, I was here all night.
You're the best friend I ever had.
No, I'm not busy.
Tell me if I'm boring you.
I'm sorry. I feel like I've been doing all the talking.

And more

I'm never too busy for you.

I'd love to come. You know how I feel about Czechoslovakian folk dancing. But I'm afraid that I'm busy that night.

Ha ha ha. What ever gave you the idea that I don't like William?

There's nothing we can't discuss.

You know I didn't mean it.

Inseparable.

You won't hurt my feelings.

Whatever you want to do.

It's not up to me.

Friends of yours are having a dinner party. The last time you went to a dinner party at their house, you were seated next to a man who blamed the recent discovery of ground glass in babyfood on a Communist conspiracy and a man who taught you the ins and outs of plastic containers. You would rather spend the night in Spud-U-Like on your own than go to another dinner party at your friends' house. You say

Just try to keep me away.

What everyone says when they can't do something they didn't want to do

Oh, what a shame. I really would have liked that.

Your best friend has a new boyfriend. This is the first serious relationship she's had since her last boyfriend went out for a newspaper three years ago and never came back. She's been talking about this new man for weeks. Terence Trent D'Arby should be so attractive. Sting should be so intelligent. Bob Geldof should be so kind. Oddly enough, the rock star he reminds you of most is Ozzy Osbourne. As soon as you get home, your friend phones. 'Well?' she squeals. 'What did you think? Isn't he the sweetest, nicest man you've ever met?'

Yes.

Yes, he's wonderful.

I'm so jealous.

What a honey.

Aren't you lucky.

Does he have a brother?

For your birthday, your friend gives you something that is too small, too old fashioned and the wrong colour

Oh . . . wow . . .
I love it.
This is fantastic.
This is the best present I've ever had.
It's just what I always wanted.
No, really.
You always know just what to get me.
I can really put this to good use.
It must be synchronisity. I was just saying the other day . . .

To which your friend replies

I just knew you'd like it.
You're sure you like it? You wouldn't lie to me, would you?
I kept the receipt. You can always take it back.
I won't be upset if you want to exchange it.

Lies between friends when one of them has had a sudden success, stroke of luck, or wins the pools

I'm so happy for you!
This is just great.
It couldn't have happened to a better person.
I'm as pleased for you as I would be for myself.
You really deserve it.
Oh, come on, I could never be jealous of a friend.

In order for the Worthwells – Frank, Anna and their three children, Beowulf, Ariel and baby Ludmilla – to stay with you while their ground floor is being pumped out, a few adjustments have to be made in the life of your own family. The girls have to move in together so Beowulf, who is a very sensitive child, has a room to himself. Your boy has to sleep on the couch so Ariel, who is also sensitive, in her way, has somewhere to sleep. You and your husband have to move in with your toddler so Frank, Anna and Ludla ('Yes,' you cooed, 'it's an adorable nickname') have a room of their own, Ludla

being something of a night person. In addition, the Worthwells' children are not allowed to eat the toxic junk you permit your children to eat. Their eating habits are environmentally sound. Thus, for obvious reasons (the Worthwell children, unlike your children, have delicate natures and would be upset by the sight of your children stuffing their faces with chips and chocolate bars and, Lord help us, hamburgers) a few changes have to be made to the menu as well. By the end of the 'few days' – three weeks, four days, six hours and seventeen minutes your family is noticeably thin, pale, wan, and tetchy. As the Worthwells all climb into their Land Rover, smiling and waving, Anna calls out, 'I hope we weren't any trouble.' Your husband and children keep waving and smiling. You say

Of course not.

A few days later you are talking to Anna Worthwell on the telephone. 'You know,' she says, 'Frank and I and the children really miss you. Staying with you was so much fun.' You swallow the last bit of your chocolate, peanut butter and tunafish sandwich and say

Oh, we miss you, too.

The lies your friend tells you when s/he has to stay with you while the builders are in

It'll only be for a couple of days.

Please, I want you to promise to tell me if I'm in the way.

I can always move into a hotel.

I couldn't remember where it went.

Oh, isn't that the rag for the floor?

I hope we didn't make too much noise . . .

Gee whiz, how did that happen?

I knew you wouldn't mind if I asked Douglas in for a drink.

There wasn't much left.

I'm not really allergic.

Oh, no, I wasn't cold.

I thought it was electric.

Of course I don't mind if you're entertaining. I can go out.

I thought you said you had more.

I'll replace it.
I'm sure it was scratched already.

You must let me give you some money . . .
You won't even know I'm here.

The lies you tell your friend when s/he has to stay with you while the builders are in

I just love having you.
It's so much fun having someone else around all the time.
No trouble at all.
As long as you like.
Don't be ridiculous, I wouldn't hear of it.
Feel free . . .

Oh no, it's nice to see the good dishes used more.
It's my fault, I should have told you . . .
He's only a dog.
He's only a child.
It can be fixed.
Oh, did you come in late?

The lie your best friend tells you about the blind date he's arranged for you with his accountant

I just know you're going to hit it off.

The two greatest friend lies

Tell me the truth.
I will.

Every summer your friend, Annie, goes to Greece for three weeks. Every year she promises to send you a postcard. Every year she doesn't. You accuse her of lying about going to Greece and really going to Luton instead. She says, 'Don't be ridiculous.' You say, 'Well, why don't you ever send me a card?' She says

But I did.
They must have been lost in the post.
You mean you never got my letter?
I never send anybody a card.
I think I must have the wrong address for you.

You and your friend have been planning to go to the Bahamas together. Everything's been arranged. You've got a great deal on the flight. There's a convention of models staying in the same hotel. And as you are the millionth guests, the hotel is giving you your room for free. The day before you're scheduled to depart, you break your leg. Your friend offers to stay home and nurse you. You say

No, no, you go without me.
Have a good time.
Of course, I'll be fine.
I'm sure I don't mind.

Drinking lies

I'm not drunk.
Just one.
Just one more.
Only to be sociable.
It helps me relax.
It doesn't affect me.
I can take it or leave it.
But it tastes just like chocolate.

Whew, what did you put in that
    punch? I only had one glass
    and, the next thing you know,
    I'm speaking in Spanish.
I'm never going to get drunk
    again so long as I live.
This time I really mean it.

At 6 a.m. the police arrive at the garden shed behind the pub, where a party seems to be going on. When asked for an explanation, the publican says

They all bought their drinks before closing time, officer.
We're just having a pre-match tipple.

Smokers' lies

It relaxes me.
Only when I'm nervous.
Only when I'm drinking.
I don't inhale.
I could give up any time.
I'm quitting next week.
I quit.

You forgot your friend's birthday. You say

You mean you didn't get my card?
It must have got lost in the post.
You mean you're a *Libra*?
Why do I always think your birthday's in the spring?
Oh, I knew it was coming up soon.
I had it written down and everything.
I couldn't decide what to get you.
I wanted to surprise you with something really special.
I ordered something weeks ago . . .
Gee whiz, I left it at home.
Wait till you see what I got you.

Your friend forgot your birthday. You say

I hate birthdays.
I want to forget it anyway.
Oh, for heaven's sake, I wasn't expecting anything . . .
It doesn't matter.

Your friend gives you a Christmas present, as you were expecting he would. You say

You shouldn't have.

You hate it. You tell yourself

It's the thought that counts.

You tell him

I love it.
No, I really do.
I'd never have the nerve to buy something like this for myself.
It's the sort of thing you can only get as a gift, isn't it?

Your friend has a Christmas present for you; but you don't have one for him. You say

I have one for you.
I left it at home.
It hasn't come yet.
You know what mail order is like.
Now, where did I put it . . .
I wanted to get you something really special.

Your friend says

You didn't have to.

You have a Christmas present for your friend; but he doesn't have one for you. You say

Oh don't worry, it isn't much.
Oh, please, it doesn't matter.
I wasn't expecting anything.
I hate presents.
I was hoping you wouldn't get me anything.

Great guest lies

I'm sorry I'm late.
Traffic.
All I want is a cup of tea.
Harry was so sorry he couldn't make it.
I got lost.
Oh, no it wasn't your directions.
I'd be happy to pay for it.
My fault entirely.
You must give me the recipe.
This is delicious.
I had a big lunch.
I love mussels.
I love dogs.
I love children.
No, no, I love cats.
I really prefer to sit on the floor.
No, I'm fine. Really.
I hope I'm not boring you.

Don't worry about it, it's an old jacket.
I have such a small appetite.
I just wasn't hungry.
What interesting friends you have.
I wish I didn't have to rush off like this.
But you know what babysitters are like.
I can't remember when I've had more fun.
We must do this again soon.
Next time, you have to come to me.
I'm sure it tastes great.
I just love eating outdoors.
Please, don't let me break up the party . . .

The lie you tell your hostess when you ring the next day to thank her for the lovely evening that was largely spent in watching her and the host bat insults back and forth at one another like ping-pong players in the final round of a tournament

Oh, was there a little tension? I didn't really notice..

Classic hostess lies

It's all right, really.
Nothing like this has ever
  happened before.
It usually turns out so well.
It's French.
It's meant to look like that.
I know it doesn't look it, but it's
  actually clean.
I did exactly what the recipe
  said.
And those chairs seemed so
  sturdy.
It's an old family recipe.
Of course, I don't usually buy
  things ready-made . . .
Make yourself at home.
Do come again.
It was no trouble at all.
Don't worry about it. It's not the
  first time someone's spilt a
  bottle of Chianti on it.

Please, don't apologize.
I'm sure I can mend it.
Oh, no, we're really rather fond
  of children.
We're so sorry you couldn't
  make it.
We're so sorry you can't stay on.
There may be a tiny bit too
  much salt.
It was broken anyway.
Wake us? Oh, no, you didn't
  wake us.
It's been a pleasure.
Stay as long as you like.
Next time you must stay longer.
Just push it aside if you don't
  want to eat it. I understand.
Of course I'm not offended.
What makes you think
  anything's wrong?
It could happen to anyone.

Two classic guest lies

I wouldn't think of suing.
Just a night or two.

One classic guest lie

Just tell me when you want to go to bed.

The lies hosts tell when they want their company to leave

Oh, my goodness, look at the time! I had no idea it was so late.
We've got to get up pretty early in the morning.
I'm afraid we're out of brandy . . .
There have been an awful lot of car thefts in this neighbourhood
  recently.
I don't want to rush you or anything . . .

Lies of the guest who wants to leave without seeming impolite

This is such a great evening, but I'm afraid I have to get up at dawn.
I'm afraid the babysitter can't stay past eleven.
Oh my God, is that the time?
Doesn't time fly when you're having fun?
I've got to get home to take my medication.
Is that a car alarm I hear?
I'd better hurry if I want to catch the last train.

**This year, Geraldine and Harold's New Year's Eve party
hasn't been too bad. True, the wine is not in bottles but in
boxes. True, this year they have had it catered not by the
usual outfit but by a local Thai restaurant, which means that
though there are no cheese chunks with pineapple or baby
quiches, what you do have, although delicious, is so small and
fleeting that you find yourself thinking almost fondly of
sausage rolls and bowls of peanuts. And, true, every time a
good rock song comes on the stereo some sado-masochist
comes along and puts on Luther Van Dross. Nonetheless you
have found a few old friends to chat to, and the wine isn't so
bad after the third glass, and Geraldine and Harold's twelve-
year-old, who has always been fond of you, has given you half
of his peanut butter sandwich, so, on the whole, it beats
sitting home by yourself with a bottle of beer, worrying about
what the new year might bring. And then, just as you are
wiping the last bits of peanut butter from your mouth and
thinking about switching to red and dancing with the twelve-
year-old, along comes Alvin. Alvin is in plastics. He makes
knobs. He makes knobs for desks and dressers and radios and
cassette players and toys. You have no idea what a demand
there is for durable plastic knobs, nor how complex the
marketing network is, nor how dependent the Western world
is on plastic knobs, but you are about to find out. 'You looked
like you were about to get another drink,' says Alvin, 'what'll
it be, the New Zealand blanc de blanc or the Romanian rioja?'
You say**

I think I hear my cab.

The great host lie

Do you really have to go so soon?

The great guest lie

Yes.

Lies to an unexpected guest

What a pleasant surprise.
How nice of you to drop in.
It's so good to see you.
I've been meaning to invite you over.
No, we weren't busy.
I hope you'll be able to stay for supper.
Oh, no, of course it's all right.

Lies of an unexpected guest

I hope I'm not disturbing you.
Are you sure?
I just happened to be in the neighbourhood.
I knew you wouldn't forgive me if I didn't stop by.
I won't stay long.
Oh, I didn't mean for you to feed me . . .
Please, don't go to any trouble.
Look, if you're doing something, just tell me and I'll go.

Lies of the guest who would like to come back

That was how I found it.
What top sheet?
You must let me pay . . .
The home video of your holiday in the Lake District? Why, I can't
    think of anything I'd rather see.
Of course he didn't disturb me. I can understand that he thinks of it
    as his bed. Labradors are like that, aren't they?
Oh, hey, Eric, what's a little baby vomit between friends? It'll wash
    out.

Great party lies

I thought you looked familiar.
Didn't we meet at Jeff's last party?
And what do you do for a living, Michael? My goodness, isn't that
    fascinating.
I'm sorry, I don't dance.
Warm? No, I'm not warm.
It is a bit stuffy in here, isn't it?
What a great party.

The lie everyone makes when they first see someone's new baby

Oh, isn't it sweet?

Followed by

He looks just like you.
I don't think her ears are big.
She has her daddy's smile.
Really? And then what happened?

The lie everyone tells you when you go to see their new baby

I'm sorry to keep going on about him like this. I hope I'm not boring
    you.

To which the traditional response is

Oh no, you're not boring me at all. What happened after your water
    broke?

Dog owners' lies

Man's best friend.
I'm sure he won't do it again.
There's nothing to be afraid of.
He's just being friendly.
He must really like you.
He's never done anything like
    that before.
It must be something she smells
    on you.
You must have cats.
They can tell if you're afraid.
She never bites.
Just give him a shove.
I wouldn't say he sheds exactly.

He doesn't go to just anyone.
I know she looks ferocious, but
   she's really very friendly.

If you just stand still . . .
He's almost human.

HE'S ALMOST HUMAN.

Cat owners' lies

She never scratches.
I don't usually allow him on the
   furniture.
It means he likes you.
Oh, my goodness. Now what
   made her do a thing like that?
You must have frightened him.
She always uses her litter tray.
They're so clean.

They're so intelligent.
They're so affectionate.
They're so independent.
It's probably just a hairball.
Did I forget to warn you about
   that chair?
I knew you wouldn't mind.
I'm sure she didn't mean to.
She doesn't mean anything by it.

**The lie Marcia Clearwater told when you put your foot in the
cat litter tray that, unbeknownst to you, was under your chair**

I meant to move it.

The lie the cat owner tells his guests when the cat lands on the turkey in the middle of dinner

She's never done anything like that before.

Lies pet owners tell you when they give you their pets to mind while they go to Crete

He won't be any trouble.
He never barks.
You can leave him alone for hours.
I'll leave you plenty of food.
Of course I wouldn't hold you responsible . . .
She's so good with children.
He's a great mouser.
Totally trained.
You can't overfeed them.
It takes about five minutes.
He practically walks himself.
He always comes back.
He's not going to pull out all his feathers.
She'll come out when she's hungry.
She's not like other Siamese cats.
You just mash up the pills in her food.
The eye drops are easy to put in.
She actually likes the medication .
He eats anything.
Of course not. They've got their scratching pole with them.

Lies your friends tell you when they ask you to water their plants while they're in Crete

There's nothing to it.
Just a couple.
Once a week.
You'll be able to tell.
I'll leave clear instructions.
They're not going to die overnight.

Lies your friends tell you when they ask you to mind their child while they go away for the weekend

He won't be any trouble.
You know how fond he's always been of you.
She never gets homesick.
She'll eat whatever you eat.
He's always well behaved with other people.
She isn't fussy.
Just treat him like he's your own.
It's just a little cold.

Classic housework lies

I was just about to do it.
It must have been the dog.
It's a very dusty part of town.
You wouldn't think I cleaned
    the whole place for you
    yesterday, would you?
You can't really notice.
You could eat on her floor.
I could never sleep in an untidy
    room.
I've got a bad back.
I can't reach that high.
It won't come out.
I can't throw it out. It might
    come in handy someday.
There's something wrong with
    the Hoover.
I can't find the mop.
There aren't enough cupboards.
A bomb just hit it.
It's the maid's day off.

More great party lies

It's going to be really wild.
You're going to have the time of
    your life.
Everybody will be there.
Plenty of food.
Plenty to drink.
It'll go on for days.
The neighbours are fine.
We've never had to call the
    cops yet.
There won't be any gate-
    crashers.
It won't be the same without
    you.

I guarantee you're going to meet
    someone really wonderful this
    time.
Of course there'll be dancing.
Bring whoever you want.
He's not going to be there.
There's someone I've been
    wanting you to meet.
Come as late as you like.
Don't you just love these little
    things wrapped in pastry?
Yes.
You'll be sorry you missed it.

And more

It's the best party I've ever been to.

What a terrific crowd.

Your friends from work are so entertaining.

Oh, no, of course I'm not offended. He's really very funny.

Oh, goody, salt and vinegar crisps.

It's all right, really. I ate before I left the house.

I didn't really want a beer anyway.

Angela, really, the dip's terrific.

Maybe they got the wrong night.

Boy, I never would have thought of dancing to the soundtrack from *South Pacific*.

I'm sorry I have to go so soon.

Thank you, but I already have a lift home.

Haven't we met before?

Of course I haven't had too much to drink.

I don't really remember what happened after that . . .

You're really a great dancer.

It could happen to anyone.

I'm sure no one noticed.

I'm fine to drive home.

I don't usually smoke . . .

This is so much fun.

I'm never going to another party again so long as I live.

No, this time I really mean it.

See, what did I tell you? That wasn't so bad.

Overhearing the conversation of the couple standing by the miniature quiches, which largely consists of him explaining to her the course he went on to improve his memory, you start laughing so much that you begin to choke. When your hostess asks if you're all right you say

Oh fine, fine. Something went down the wrong way.

You meet someone at a party who seems to be rather taken with you. Not, sadly, a mutual state of affairs. This person asks you to dance. You say

The ankle hasn't healed yet.

I don't really dance.

I can't dance to this.

I think my date's looking for me.

I'm pretty pooped out from the charades.

Maybe later.

This person asks you to stroll in the garden. You say

I think they've got rats.
I'm not much of a walker.
I'm allergic to grass. Yes, it's very inconvenient.

This person asks for your telephone number

I'm not on the phone.
Oh, absolutely. Remind me to give it to you before I leave.
It's in the book.
I can't remember it. You give me yours and I'll ring you tomorrow.

The lies you tell your neighbours the day after the party

Gate-crashers.
I'm really sorry.
You can believe it'll never happen again.
I'm sure that none of my guests did that.

The lies you tell the party's host the next day when you phone up to get the telephone number of the girl you were sharing the yoghurt and spring onion dip with, who seemed reluctant to give it to you herself

I just rang to thank you for the great party.
You know? Well, I promised I'd ring her with the name of a good
    homeopath but I can't find the napkin I wrote her number down
    on. You wouldn't happen to have her number, would you?

Telephone lies

I just got in.
I was just going out.
I was just about to step into the
    bath.
I'll have to ring you back,
    someone wants to use the
    phone.
I just got out of the shower.

I'll call you right back.
She's in the tub.
He's gone to Brighton.
He'll be back in an hour.
We were just about to eat.
Look, darling, I'm afraid I'm a
    little tied up right now . . .
Of course I'm alone.

Can you hear me? Really? I'm
  getting a terrible buzz . . .
I know I've got your number.
I was here all night. I never
  heard it ring.

We've had a lot of trouble on the
  line.
I never got the message.
I did ring back but the line was
  engaged.

The reason the telephone bill is so high

There's something wrong with the meter.

What you say when you answer the telephone and a voice you don't recognize greets you with an enthusiastic 'Hi! It's me!'

Well, hi! How've you been?

The reason the little red light on your answering-machine isn't flashing when you come back from a long weekend away

There's something wrong with the machine.

Other answering-machine lies

No one's here at the moment to take your call.
Someone will ring you right back.
Gee, I never got your message.
There's something wrong with the machine.
The kids must have erased it.
I don't talk to machines.

Borrowers' lies

I'll bring it right back.
Just overnight.
Oh, gosh, I forgot it again.
I wish you'd reminded me.
I even wrote myself a note.
You mean, that's your drill?
I must apologize for keeping it
  so long.
Of course I'll replace it . . .
I'm sure I returned it.

I used to have one that looked
  just like it.
Normally, I wouldn't ask,
  but . . .
I can't tell you how much I
  appreciate this.
As long as you're sure you
  don't mind.
It was like that already.
You must let me pay you.

Lenders' lies

I'd forgotten all about it.
Oh, that's where it was.
No, really, it always tilted to the left like that.
Oh, no, I couldn't expect you to replace it.
I can't find it or you'd be welcome to use it.
It wasn't expensive.
Keep it as long as you like.
I wouldn't ask for it back if it weren't for the fact that . . .

Your friend has lent you a considerable sum of money (say more than ten pounds and less than a million). Both of you know you can't really afford to pay it back, and probably never had any intention of doing so. You say

Now look, Albert, I insist on paying back every penny.
How about five pounds a week?
No, I really can't accept such generosity.
I have my pride.
I know it'll take me a while . . .
How will I ever be able to thank you?

Third-bottle-of-wine lies

You're the best friend I've ever had.
No one else really understands me.
I'm not just saying this because I'm drunk.
This'll be the last.

Drivers' lies

There's nothing to be nervous about.
I knew it was a 'give way'.
There wasn't anything coming, was there?
I knew he was going to stop.
They always squeal like that.
It certainly wasn't my fault.
Well, look where they hide the sign . . .
I thought it was a roundabout.
I forgot it was a roundabout.
Of course there's a jack in the boot.
Did you see how close he got to me?

I was only doing thirty.
There was nothing coming.
He just jumped out at me.
Well, nobody ever told me.
I thought you said left.
I did look.
He waved me on.
I never lose my temper behind
the wheel.

I don't know, I guess I just got
nervous when he started
beeping his horn like that.
I forgot.
Everybody else does.
It wasn't my fault.
Officer, I have a good reason.

Your friend Alicia calls you up one evening, after the theatre is out, in a right old tizzy. 'You won't believe it!' she screams. 'I've been clamped!' 'Clamped'! you exclaim. 'Oh, no. What happened?' 'That's what happened,' says Alicia. 'I was parked at a meter, it was after eight, everything was absolutely legal and fine, and I came out two hours later and there's a big yellow thing attached to the wheel of my car.' 'Where was this?' you ask, perplexed, thinking perhaps that she was in another country where the laws are different for the evening. 'In town,' shouts Alicia. 'Can you believe it? Right in the middle of town. At a meter!' 'But I don't understand it,' you say. 'Why would they clamp you if you were at a meter?' 'Fascists,' says Alicia. 'Vindictive fascist policemen.' You remember the time Alicia drove you to the cinema and parked on the pavement because all the spaces on the street were already taken. 'Uh, Alicia,' you say carefully, 'you weren't too close to the kerb, were you?' She says

Of course not.

The great driving lie

Women drivers.

Learning to drive a car lies

All you need is a little practice.
Everybody makes that mistake the first few times.
Of course I'm not nervous.
My students always pass.

The six great lies you tell everyone after you fail your driving test

I was nervous.
I was tired. The baby kept me up the night before.
The examiner didn't like me.
They always fail you the first time.
It didn't say one way.
I must have practised too much.

Lies your friends tell you when you fail your driving test

They always fail you the first time.
You'll pass next time, no problem.
I can't understand it.
He must have had a bad day.
Well, that's what I'd do at a roundabout.
It could happen to anyone.

School lies

I had a stomach ache.
I left it at home.
My mother was sick.
I was sick.
The baby ate it.
The dog ate it.
The teacher doesn't like me.
No reason.
I do listen.

I do my homework.
I did do my homework.
I lost it.
It fell through a hole in the floor
    of the car.
Of course I studied.
I just can't understand what
    happened. I worked so hard.

You're tired of sitting around like an old potato on the couch every evening. You decide to take an adult education class. Learn something new. Broaden your horizons. Accomplish something. Make new friends. Of course, you haven't forgotten the fifty-six other evening classes, including beginner's Serbo-Croat, that you've taken in the past. Or that only two of them lasted more than three weeks. To get around

the nagging thought that this might be number fifty-seven, you tell yourself that

This time it's going to be different.
I'm not giving up, no matter what.

Lies you tell your instructor

I won't miss much.
I know what I'm doing.
Oh, yes, I understand now.
I've been ill.
I really don't feel that you explained it clearly.
I'll make it up.
Wednesdays? No, I can't make Wednesdays.

Lies your instructor tells you

Five lessons, that's all you'll need.
This is so easy . . .
This is so easy once you know how . . .
No, really, you're doing quite well.
You'll get there in the end.
There's nothing to be afraid of.
Of course no one's going to force you . . .

Most people learn to do this in about thirty minutes.
It's all in the wrist.
You'll get the hang of it.
Anyone can do it.
You don't have to be athletic . . .
It isn't a question of size . . .
Age doesn't matter . . .
In just a week or two you'll notice the difference.
It could happen to anyone.

The reasons people are late

They're sorry.
The clock stopped.
They didn't realize we'd gone off daylight saving time.
Traffic.
The car.
Just as they were leaving the house, the telephone started to ring . . .
You mean you didn't say nine forty-five?

They had to stop for petrol.
It gets a little tricky after that second light, doesn't it?
They had to go back to make sure the iron had been turned off.
They had to go back to make sure they double-locked the door.
They forgot the wine.
Something came up.
They must have dozed off.
They knew you'd understand.

The reasons people don't turn up at all

Oh my God, did you mean *this* Sunday?
The baby's come down with the 'flu.
The car won't start.
They thought their uncle was arriving on Saturday.
The cat went missing.
They must have dozed off.

What you say when your guests phone two hours after you expected them, to tell you how sorry they are and that they have a really good excuse even though they know you're not going to believe them

Of course I will
See, I told you I would.
Don't be silly, it could happen to anyone.
The soufflé will keep, believe me.
It doesn't matter.
Nothing to apologize for.
Oh, yes, of course we must arrange another date.

The great polite conversation lie

How could I be bored?

Variations of the great polite conversation lie

No, it's fascinating.
You don't mean it?
Really?

And then what?
Well, I must say, I'm just
   amazed.

I've always wondered how they got them into those little bottles.
Isn't that interesting?
Oh, no, please go on.

Would you excuse me for just a second? There's someone over there I have to talk to urgently.

You run into an old acquaintance at a cocktail party. 'Well, hello,' you say. 'Well, hello,' says she. While you are saying, 'And how have you been?' her eyes are focused on someone more interesting behind you. Without ever answering your question, she waves to that more interesting person and prepares to join them. Bumping into you on her way past, she says

Nice talking to you.

You run into an old acquaintance at a cocktail party. 'Hey, there,' you cry. 'How have you been? Long time no see.' It is relatively clear from the expression on your acquaintance's face, as blank as the screen of a broken television, that he does not remember you with the clarity with which you remember him. He says

It's been ages. What are you up to now?
How long has it been?
Still living in the same place?

The lies the man next door told upon being found in the back garden in his pyjamas at one in the morning

I was calling the cat and the door slammed behind me.
I thought I heard a noise.

The lies the man next door told upon being discovered shimmying up the drainpipe at two in the morning, holding his briefcase in his mouth, and with the distinct aroma of gold tequila clinging to his person

I forgot my key.
The doorbell's broken.
My wife's a very heavy sleeper.

The three lies told by the man next door when you found him sleeping in the back of his car at seven in the morning

I forgot my key.
The doorbell's broken.
My wife's a very heavy sleeper.

Lies neighbours tell each other

We didn't hear a thing.
It was enough to wake the dead.
It wasn't us.
It's temporary.
We won't be away more than a
   day or two . . .
He won't get out again.
Oh, is that your cat?

I'm sure it couldn't have been
   Tigger.
I'm sure it couldn't have been
   Johnny.
Sure, I'll keep an eye on it.
Nothing like this has ever
   happened before.
It doesn't matter.

Lies people tell the Jehovah's Witnesses

I was just going out.
I'm on the phone.
If you could come back on Wednesday . . .
Oh, yes, I couldn't agree with you more.
I've left something on the stove.
I'm afraid I'm busy right now.

Lies people tell the woman collecting for Greenpeace outside the chemist's

I don't have any change right now.
We're late for a wedding.
I'll catch you on the way back.
We're just tourists.
I already gave.
I lost my sticker.

Lies people tell the Greenpeace volunteer who is standing on the doorstep

We already gave.
I'm on the phone right now.
I've got a house full of guests.
We just sat down to eat.
I don't have any change.
This isn't my house.
I'm on my way out.
I support that other organization.

Reasons for not contributing to the collection for Mary's wedding/birthday/leaving present at the office

I hardly know her.
She wouldn't remember me.
I haven't got any change right now. I'll give it to you after lunch.
Don't you remember? I already gave.
Mary? Is she getting married again?
Well, I wouldn't say we were really _close_.
Who?

Reasons for not giving blood at the office

I'm anaemic.
I always forget to sign up.
I'll be out of town that day. Worse luck.
I would if I could, but . . .

Why you don't turn up for the office Christmas party, even though you said you would

Cramps.

Angela calls you about every six months, usually when she's pissed as a newt. Angela can talk for two and a half hours (this is not her record but her average) without having to take time out for anything as distracting as taking a pee, getting a cup of tea, breathing, or asking you anything about yourself. It is not that you don't like Angela, you tell your other friends, you do appreciate what a nice person she is, really, deep down, underneath, but she can be a bit wearing. Her life, after all, is not any more interesting than yours – in fact, as far as you're concerned, it's a lot less interesting. And she does, it is true, tend to talk about the same thing over and over. Her boyfriend Elwood. After an acquaintance of six years it is difficult to be sympathetic about her problems with Elwood. Despite the fact that you can't help feeling that probably even Elwood doesn't deserve Angela, the advice you would like to give her is, 'Shoot him.' Your six months are up. You climb down from the scaffolding to answer the phone (you are painting a jungle mural on the ceiling of your bedroom) and find yourself sitting there for 105 minutes as the paint dries above you and the brush in your hand goes hard while Angela tearfully and slightly slurrily tells you what Elwood has done this time (which is not that much different, of course, from what he did last time). In the split second pause between sobs you say

The creep.

In the next nanosecond pause you say

You poor thing.

Three hours later, when you have resigned yourself to the fact that you couldn't have done much more tonight anyway, not until you've bought a new brush, Angela says, 'I'm sorry for banging on like this. It must be so boring.' You say

Don't be ridiculous, you're my friend,
or alternatively,
Don't be ridiculous, I'm only too happy to help.
or maybe even
I know you'd do the same for me.

You're strolling down the street on a Saturday afternoon, doing the weekend errands – which include finding out why the dry cleaner's doesn't have your rugs yet (they'll be ready Monday), why the turntable isn't ready yet (come back Monday), and why you're not going to make cheese lasagne for dinner after all (they won't have any ricotta till Monday), when you spy a familiar figure coming towards you. Much as you like her, you are not in the mood to stand on the corner for forty-five minutes while Marcia Clearwater tells you all about her latest diet. As soon as she says, 'Did I tell you I haven't eaten anything but artichokes for the last thirteen days?' you say

Oh, Marcia, I'd love to stay and chat, but . . .
I'm in a terrible rush.
I've got to pick up the kids.
I'm double parked.
Harry's waiting in the car. You know what he's like.
I just remembered I left the iron on.
Artichokes! Oh, my God, I left something on the stove.

Marcia says that the two of you must get together soon. You say

Oh, yes. That would be great.
I'll ring you.
Give me a call.
Can't wait.
Look forward to it.
Very, very soon.

Marcia invites you to supper on Monday. You say

I think I might be busy. I'll let you know.
Oh, shucks, that's the night of my pottery class.
Monday? Oh, wow, I've got this date I made three months ago . . .
What a pity, Monday's the one night I can't make.
Besides Tuesday.

Reasons people give for not going to places they don't want to go to, doing things they don't want to do, or eating artichokes with people they don't feel like eating artichokes with

I'll just check my diary . . . Oh, what a shame.
Teriffic. I'll be there. Oh, wait a minute, You don't mean *this* Tuesday, do you.
Oh, I'd really love to, but . . .
I've had this awful cold.
If I'm feeling better I'd love to come. These things do hang on, though, don't they?
I wouldn't want you to catch it.
The children may be coming down with the 'flu.
You're not going to believe this, Edwina, but the car won't start.
I've got this migraine.
I was sure I'd be feeling better by now.
I can't leave the cat.
I'm not sure what Harry's doing.
Something's come up.
I can't really explain on the phone.
You know what this job of mine's like . . .
I've got house-guests for the next three weeks.
You'd hate them.
I'll ring you next week.
I'm on this special diet . . .
My babysitter's gone to Yugoslavia for the next six months.

What the person who's inviting you says when he or she won't take no for an answer

But I had to cancel the Thatchers because of you.
Well how about Wednesday, then?
That doesn't matter, bring them along.
That doesn't matter I'm sure we'll find something for you to eat.
So you're a few hours late . . .
We'll meet you there. You don't need us to find the way.

In the end, you have to concoct a story that involves a man from Texas, a chimpanzee, a truckload of oranges and the greatest rock and roll band in the world. 'I know this must sound as if I'm making it up,' you say to the person who has unwisely asked you over for dinner. She says

Oh no, not at all.

Wedding lies

Every bride is beautiful.
White wedding.
Don't worry honey, it'll go
   without a hitch.
Of course we'll be on time.
Isn't she lovely?
No, I didn't come with
   anyone . . .
You only get married once.

I did say there was a certain
   flexibility to the catering
   costs.
The delivery van's broken down.
No one will notice.
He's on his way.
Wasn't that wonderful?
I don't think anyone noticed.

You come home from work on a Friday evening after a day that would have given Indiana Jones a challenge. If possible, you feel even worse than you look. All you want to do is pour yourself a glass of cold wine, slip into a hot bath, and then curl up with a good video and a box of biscuits. Instead, you've been sitting in a draughty coffee bar with your best friend for the last two hours, trying to advise her on what dress to wear to dinner with her boyfriend's boss and pretending that you don't know why she won't let you go

**home. As you walk into the flat the lights suddenly go on and
thirty of your closest friends, dust bunnies clinging to them,
jump up from behind the furniture shouting, 'Surprise!
Surprise! ' You say**

Oh, you shouldn't have [this, of course, is not a factual lie, but one
  that is more a matter of tone].
What a surprise!
This is the best birthday I've ever had.
I can't tell you how touched I am.
What a great bunch of friends.
Oh, I love surprises!

Your best friend, who has organized this for you, says

I knew you'd like it.
I knew you'd never guess.

You say

I can't thank you enough.

**You've gone out to dinner with a few friends to celebrate your
birthday. You're sitting there, waiting for the waiter to
reappear with the meal you actually ordered this time, when
suddenly this guy in a loincloth hovers into view. Much to
your amazement, he marches up to you, lifts you out of your
chair, flings you over his shoulder, and parades around the
other diners singing, 'Happy birthday to you, happy birthday
to you, happy birthday Susan Winterbottom of Seventeen
Seagrove Crescent, happy birthday to you . . .' After you've
been returned to your seat, your friends say**

Wasn't that hilarious?
We knew you'd get a kick out of it.
You're such a good sport.

You say

Thanks.
What cards.
I guess that was something to tell my grandchildren.

Someone gives you a present you hate. You want to take it back. You say

Of course I like it.
It's not that I don't like it.
It's a great colour, but on me . . .
I know you'd want me to be honest with you . . .
What a shame, Larry gave me one just like it.
I know it's my size, but it's cut small.
I know just the place for it . . .

There is one slice of German chocolate cake (arguably the best chocolate cake ever made in this galaxy) left. But there are two people sitting at the table. You say

No, really, you have it. I'm absolutely stuffed.

'We could share it,' says your dining companion, though not with much conviction. You say

No, really, I'm on a diet.

'Well,' says your friend, 'If you're sure . . .' You say, graciously

Well, if you insist.

Lies between children

Your mother's never going to
  find out.
I'm going to tell.
I'm not going to tell.
My mother lets me do anything
  I want.
Scared? Me?
Mine's better.
I've got one just like it.

I'd rather be a nice person than
  pretty and popular and stuck
  up like her.
I knew that.
I swear it's the truth.
Why would I lie?
I don't care
I didn't really want it anyway.

What your friends say when you're on the local radio talking about how you started your world-famous tea-towel collection

Can you believe it? I completely forgot it was on!
I couldn't find the station.
I must've dozed off.
I thought you sounded great.
Completely natural.
It wasn't your fault he asked such stupid questions.
I'm sure you were wonderful.
Oh, don't be silly. Nobody was laughing at you.
Was that you?

General out-in-the-world lies

This seat is taken.
I'm waiting for someone.
I was here first.
Oh no you weren't.
They're coming right back.
I won't be a minute.
You're next.
It's not mine.
I'll come back for it later.
Everybody does it.

3
Men, Women, Sex, Love and Lies

Not even politics, law, business, the communications industry or estate agents, none of whom are particularly known for their close association with the truth, have thrown so many great lies on the market as have love, sex and old-fashioned lust. It's almost as though on that fateful day in the garden of Eden when the words 'What apple?' were spoken the entire course of human relationships was irrevocably set. Don't tell the truth if you can possibly think of something else to say. For from the first 'Isn't that fascinating?' to the last 'I'll never forget you', the lustful, the moonstruck, the disenchanted, and those trying to maintain a mature, sensible union all lie through their teeth. We lie to meet each other, to get rid of each other, to seduce each other, and to break the spell of love. We lie to keep each other, to impress each other, to please one another, to avoid arguments, to start arguments and sometimes, even, to get away with murder. The bed of love is a bed of lies. Or, to put it another way, the road that winds in and out of love is not so much rocky as paved with deceit. Which means that the old saying 'A naked man has nothing to hide' isn't true either.

You're surprised?

Love's lies

True love.
Kismet.
Destiny.
Love means never having to say you're sorry.
Absence makes the heart grow fonder.

Mr Right.
All the world loves a lover.
Love makes the world go round.
Endless love.

Lovers' lies

I've never felt like this before.
I'll never feel like this again.
I can't live without you.
I'm nothing without you.
You make me complete.
I could never look at anyone else.

The best, the very best.
Never.
You.
I don't want to play games with you.
Of course I won't laugh.

The classics

I love you.
Of course I trust you, honey.

The lies lovers tell when they're caught doing something they shouldn't have done with someone they shouldn't have been doing it with

I'm not going to lie to you.
She's just a good friend.
She's like a sister.
He's like a brother.
It was just that one time.
I thought you'd understand.
I thought you knew.
You always agreed that we shouldn't own one another.
It's not what you think.
It's not the way it looks.
If you'll just let me explain.
I never meant for this to happen.
I just couldn't help myself.
I was drunk.

It was one of those things.
It'd been so long since I'd seen you . . .
A man gets these urges.
It didn't mean anything.
I don't know how it happened.
She seduced me.
You know what happens when someone blows in my ear.
But I didn't enjoy it.
It doesn't count.
I don't even remember her/his name.
There's no reason for you to get so upset.

You have to go away for the week on business, leaving your one true love at home all by himself. 'Now don't forget,' you say to him, 'there's a pizza and those fried mushrooms you like so much in the freezer, and there's a tin of lasagne I made specially for you.' 'You're an angel,' he says, kissing your forehead. 'What did I ever do to deserve someone like you? But you know I'm never really hungry when you're away.' 'You've got to eat,' you say. 'And Bob and Ellen said they might want to go to a movie on Saturday night.' 'Aw, honey,' he says, that sad little look coming into his beautiful grey eyes, 'you know it's not the same when you're not around.' 'You can't just sit around the house by yourself,' you say. 'There's the video,' he says. 'There's solitaire. And anyway, I've got a lot of work to do.' 'You won't forget your vitamins?' you say as they call your plane. 'I won't forget.' 'I'll call you as soon as I get to the hotel,' you promise. 'I'll count the minutes,' says your own true love. As luck would have it, though, you never get to the hotel. Fog closes the airport of your destination and the plane is forced to put down in Dublin instead. You wait three hours for a flight back home. I won't call him, you tell yourself, I'll surprise him. As luck would also have it, there is some trouble with the buses back home and it takes several hours before you finally arrive at your own door. You walk into the flat, expecting to see your one true love sitting in front of the television, eating something that isn't good for him and looking lonely, but all is quiet. 'Honey!' you call. There is a red high heel on the sofa that isn't usually part of the decor. 'Honey!' you call, walking softly towards the bedroom. You open the bedroom door. There, in your bed, is your one true love and some woman you've never seen before. She, because of her position on the bed, sees you first. She gasps. Your own true love turns around. He says

This isn't the way it looks.

As you bang out of the house, he, a raincoat clutched around him, runs after you shouting

But darling, you know you're the one I love.

The lie used by approximately eighty million soldiers, doctors, sailors, politicians, musicians, artists, film-makers, actors, and rock stars over the centuries

It's a hazard of the occupation.

Lies lovers tell when they're caught thinking something they shouldn't be thinking

He's not really my type.
Does she? That's funny, I never
    noticed.
Of course you're the most attractive man/woman I know.
Of course not. I'd never even think of such a thing.
I bet she's frigid.
I bet he's in and out like a cuckoo in a clock.
It never even occurred to me.
I was thinking about getting the gutters cleaned.

Six of the very best lovers' lies

You mean you don't trust me?
There was something in her eye.

And you believed her?
It'll never happen again.
You're the last person in the world I wanted to hurt.
Well, you didn't get it from me.

Pick-up lies

You remind me of someone I used to know.
I have seen you before, haven't I?
You're very familiar.
I can give you a lift home. It's right on my way.

Lies of seduction

We won't do anything.
Just take off your top.
I'll just rub your back.
All I want is a cup of tea.
Well you can't go home in this storm, can you?

We'll just sleep together, like friends.
Of course this is special.
I've never done anything like this before.

The best lie of seduction

Then why did you invite me in for a coffee?

What Marcia Clearwater's boyfriend told her when she saw him coming out of the toilet with that blonde in the silver miniskirt at the Christmas party

I was helping her flush the loo. You know how tricky it is.

What your lover says when you want to know why he didn't show up for your date three nights ago

I hate possessive women.
Jealousy doesn't become you.
I can't believe you don't trust me.
But why, are you mad?

Night-before lies

Of course I'll still respect you.
It's not just your body I'm after.
We shouldn't deny our feelings.
I think I love you.

Morning-after lies

I'll ring you.
Of course you're going to see
    me again.
What kind of person do you
    think I am?
That was wonderful.
It's a picture of my cousin.

Lies women tell men who are more amorous than they are

I've got my period.
My boyfriend's coming back any second.
We might wake my flatmate.
I haven't had the test results yet.
Oh, I'd have to know you a lot better . . .
What sort of woman do you think I am?

One of the men at work has been pursuing you determinedly for the past few weeks. You began by being polite ('It's nice of you to offer to take me bowling on Saturday night, Derek, but I'm busy'), moved to pretty honest, ('I think we should just be friends'), and have now hit absolutely directly honest, ('Derek, I am not going out with you'). After an entire day of Derek following you around, asking for your telephone number, you finally give it to him just so you can get some work done. 'But it isn't going to do you any good, Derek,' you tell him, 'because I AM NOT GOING OUT WITH YOU. DO YOU UNDERSTAND?'

Yes. Shall I call you on Saturday?

Lies men tell women

I never hit a woman before.
You made me do it.
It's your own fault.
You asked for it.
It's different for a man.
Men have more logical minds.
Men never gossip.

Women have a natural affinity with dirty nappies that men don't have.
I can't cook.
I don't know how.
I'm just stopping off for one drink.

One of the biggest male lies of all time

All women want to be raped.

Another

Actually, I'm a feminist myself.

And another

I can't help myself. I just love women so much.

And another

Hormones.

And another

A man's gotta do what a man's gotta do.

And another

Male superiority.

You and your one true love are invited to dinner by your friends, Bob and Ellen. Ellen's nineteen-year-old niece from Australia, stopping in Britain on her way around the world, is also at dinner. Like all Australians, she is blonde, incredibly healthy-looking and unnaturally attractive. Also, like all Australians, she is good-natured, innocent, open, friendly and very warm. Bob and your one true love – kind, sensitive men who worry about young girls on their own in strange

countries – pay her a lot of attention. Before dinner they
show her the garden and the garage and they walk her around
the block. During dinner they tell her all about themselves,
information that clearly fascinates her (as, if you and Ellen
might find if you cast your minds back far enough and stopped
kicking each other under the table, it once fascinated you).
'Oh, wow,' she keeps saying. 'Oh, boy, isn't that just great?'
'Gees.' After dinner, being thoughtful and helpful like all
Australians, she offers to do the dishes. 'Why, that's very
nice,' says Ellen. But that, of course, is before Bob and your
one true love offer to help her. 'We can't have you stuck in
the kitchen all by yourself,' says your one true love, 'can we?'
'Of course we can't,' you say. 'My God,' Ellen whispers to you.
'In twenty years this is the first time either of them have ever
offered to help with the dishes.' You smile grimly. 'She must
be the wizard from Oz,' you say. After they do the dishes Bob
and your one true love challenge the niece to a computer
game. 'We could play, too,' says Ellen. 'Don't be ridiculous.'
says Bob. 'You two hate computer games.' 'No we don't,' you
say, but none of the three people jumping up and down in
front of the screen hears you. After she beats them at Battle
of the Galaxies, the men who never dance put on some music
and she shows them the latest dance craze from Sydney. Later
that night, as you and your one true love drive home, you
break the rather arctic silence with a statement about people
acting their age. One terse word leads to another and in the
end you accuse your one true love of behaving like a thirteen-
year-old. His reply to this is

I don't understand. I thought you'd want me to be nice to the poor
kid.

'Nice,' you shout, making him swerve a little sharply to the
right. 'I didn't want you to salivate all over the girl.' Your one
true love shakes his head sadly

Oh come on. You don't think I'm attracted to her do you?

Reasons for breaking a date

I have to work late.
I have to take the cat to the vet.
I can't tell you how sorry I am about this, but . . .
I've got this headache.
I've got a cold.
I think I may be coming down with the 'flu.
I was up all last night with a sick friend. I'm really whacked.
You wouldn't want to be with me when I'm like this.
All I want to do is go home and sleep.

My sister just flew in from Arizona.
I don't know how, but I totally forgot that I already had these plans . . .
I'm sure I'm contagious.
She is my only mother.
My car was just stolen.
The apartment's flooded.
I've been arrested. I'm using my one call to phone you.
I knew you'd understand.
If only I'd known. . .

What you say when someone breaks a date with you

Of course I understand.
No problem.
Oh, what a shame. Poor you.
I hope she gets better.
I hope it's nothing serious.
I've been feeling a little weak myself. There's a lot of bugs going around.
Of course it's all right.
Oh, no, I'm not upset.
I was feeling pretty tired anyway.

Well, for Pete's sake, she is your sister . . .
Oh sure, I'd love to make another date. Why don't you call me when I get back from Kenya?
Oh, goodness, I'm pretty busy myself for the next week or two. I'll give you a ring.
Don't mention it.
Don't worry about it.
It's probably just as well.

The reasons the man Marcia Clearwater met at the wedding in Kent on Sunday have her for not turning up for their lunch date on Monday

I had to fly to America.
You weren't at home.
I hate talking to answering machines.

The reason he gives you when you bump into each other in the supermarket for why he never phoned

He lost your number.
His aunt was staying with him.

Lies you tell yourself when the person you were getting on so well with at the party doesn't phone – which are also the lies you tell yourself when the person you had that great first date with never asks for another

He must have lost my number.
She must have rung while I was out.
Maybe there's something wrong with my line.
She was probably called away on business.
Maybe he had to fly to America.
Maybe he's ill.
She's probably shy.
She must have copied my number wrong.
I must have misunderstood what he said.
Maybe she didn't know I was joking.
He's forgotten my name and he's too embarrassed to call and admit it.
Maybe his mother's been taken ill and he's had to rush to her side.
He probably called while I was talking to Sally and we were on for so long that he probably decided I'd taken the receiver off the hook because I didn't really want him to call and now his feelings are hurt and he'll never phone back.

Reasons for not going out on a second date

I'm really busy at the moment.
I'm seeing someone else.
Didn't I tell you I was going on holiday?
I've just been called away on business.
I'm not going to lie to you, Harold. I think you're terrific and I had a great time at the ice hockey match, but I still haven't got over Norman.
I suddenly realized that you remind me of my mother.

I haven't been quite honest with you. You see, there is this other
    person I've been seeing . . .
I'm not ready to get into anything really serious.
I have this rare disease . . .

Romeo comes down from Glasgow to spend the weekend with Juliet. He meets her at work. He has his overnight case in his hand and signs of a gun in his pocket. He is obviously happy to see her. 'I just have to finish up one little thing,' says Juliet. 'It shouldn't take me more than half an hour.' 'That's fine,' says Romeo. 'I'll just nip around the corner and get myself something to eat.' Juliet waits an hour and a half for Romeo to return and then goes home, thinking that he must have gone there. In fact, she won't see him for three more years. The last thing he said to her was

I'll be right back.

Great beginning-of-a-relationship lies

I'm not looking for anything heavy.
No, neither am I.
I'd never try to change you.
I don't want to be rushed into anything.
Me neither.
I feel as though I'd always known you.
I've never been serious about any one before.
Let's always be honest with each other.
But it's all over now.
Not as much as I love you.
Just someone I used to date now and then.
I never think about him any more.

Great end-of-a-relationship lies

I'll never forget you.
No one will ever love you as much as I do.
Let's not have any regrets.
Of course I'm not blaming you.
You've changed.

A classic

This isn't easy.

What your lover says after he's made the crack about your hips

Don't be silly, darling, I love you the way you are.
But I like them like that.
I was only joking.
You're the one with no sense of humour.
I wouldn't get all upset if you said that to me.

One of the all-time great sex lies

I won't come in your mouth.

Another

I'll pull out, don't worry.

Lies men tell women about sex

I can tell you want it.
I can do it for hours.
It's not a problem, I'm probably sterile.
Nothing's unnatural when it comes to making love.
Of course I understand.
It's not going to hurt.
Everybody does it.
There's nothing to be ashamed of.
It's not what you've got, it's how you use it.
Just see if you like it.
Not that many.
Just tell me what you like.
I'm not one of these guys who rolls over and goes right to sleep.
What makes you think my hand's tired?
I'm surprised at you, I thought you were truly sensuous.
Now isn't this better than going to the movies?

Lies men tell men about sex

I was twelve.
Hundreds.
She was begging for it.
Can't get enough of me.
I had to stop just to give her a
    rest.
Five hours.
At least twice a day.
I get headaches if I have to go
    more than two days without
    it.
It's not what you've got, it's how
    you use it.
It's so big it's embarrassing.

Lies women tell men about sex

Yes.
I wasn't laughing.

It's not what you've got, it's how
    you use it.

I'd never fake one with you.
It happens to everyone now and then.
Of course I understand.
I've never done anything like this before.
Of course I trust you.
I didn't say I thought it was perverted . . .
Oh, yes, I really like that.

It doesn't taste bad, actually.
I almost came that time.
Nobody's blaming you.
No, honey, it's not small.
Fantastic.
The best.
Never.
It doesn't matter.
Really, it's all right.

Lies about prostitution

She's got a heart of gold.
They enjoy it.
My first time was when I was twelve in Paris.

Your paramour has been reading the letters pages of the soft porn magazines he buys for the feature articles. He comes home one night with a bag full of black underwear, most of it with holes in extraordinary places. 'Put it on, darling,' he says, 'you'll look gorgeous.' What you look like is someone whose mother would have a coronary if she saw her. What you look like is the sex fantasy of a twelve-year-old. Thank God the only boots you have are your green wellies. 'Oh wow,' says your paramour. 'Oh wow. Come over here,' he coaxes, 'let me tie you to the bed.' He straps you to the bed, cutting off circulation to your arms and causing a cramp in your right knee. 'Just sort of turn over on your side,' he says. It is very difficult to just sort of turn over on your side when your leg is attached to the bed by an old school tie and your arms are knotted onto the headboard with the belt from your dressing-gown, but you do your best. 'Sweetie,' says your paramour as he tries to squeeze himself between your head and the wall, 'isn't this great?' You say

Hmmmm.

Lies about pornography

There's nothing wrong with appreciating the human body.
It's art.
If you don't like it you don't have to look at it.
It doesn't do any harm.
Women like it as much as men.
I only buy it for the articles.

What your lover says after she's made that crack about your thinning hair

Oh, for heaven's sake, you're much too sensitive.
Bald men are sexy.
You'll still be gorgeous.

The reason why any group of men, be they construction workers, salesmen, or barristers, left by themselves in a bar will immediately start commenting on every woman who walks by with terms such as 'Varoom, varoom' and 'Look at those tits' and 'Did you see the look she gave me?'

Women expect it.
It's a compliment.
That's the way nature made them.

More lovers' lies

I'll always love you.
Forever.
I could never be mad at you.
Of course this is more than a casual fling.
I knew her before I ever met you.
You have nothing to be jealous about.
That was a long time ago.
Can't a person go out for a few hours without having to
   account for every minute?

Married men's lies

I thought you knew.
I did try to tell you.
She doesn't understand me.
She's more interested in the children.
We've simply grown apart.
She's not the jealous type.
We have an understanding.
It hasn't been good for a long time.
It's not the way it is with you.
I can't leave my children.
She depends on me.
I've tried, I've really tried.
Friday night for sure.
We'll have to ease off, my wife's getting suspicious.
I sleep with her but I don't kiss her.
Of course I didn't leave it lying around where she could find it.

The lies women tell themselves about married men

I can handle this.
I don't expect anything.
I won't get involved.
It's just one of those things.
I would never interfere with his marriage.
I can't help myself.
It's bigger than both of us.
It's got to stop.
I'm going to stop it.
Soon.
He really loves me.
He's going to tell her.
He'd leave if it weren't for the children.
It's just a matter of time.

The great ending-the-affair lies

This is goodbye.
I mean it.

Lies people tell when they don't want to have sex

I have a headache.
Really.
Boy, am I tired.
I think I'll stay up and finish this report.
You go to bed first. I'll be along in a minute.
I should never have eaten that curry.
My God, is it that late already? And I have to be up at the crack of dawn.

More than fifty lies people tell when leaving their lovers

It's not your fault.

I'm just going out for a paper, sweetheart.

It won't be for long.

I'll be back.

I'll always think of you on rainy autumn days.

I can see you're as unhappy as I am.

We can still be friends.

I don't want to hurt you.

Trial separation.

Separate vacations.

In a way, I still love you.

I'll always care about you.

You can always come to me when you're in trouble.

I thought you knew.

I need more space.

I thought you'd understand.

You love me too much.

There's no telling what she'll do if I don't go back to her.

I can't turn down a promotion like this, even if I do have to spend three years in Tahiti by myself.

This doesn't have to be the end, you know.

See you next summer.

It's not that I don't love you.
Let's just say that we've
   outgrown each other, it's
   not because she's prettier.
It's not because he's wealthy.
It's *aufwiedersehen*, not
   goodbye.
I'll write.
I'll phone every week.
We can still see each other from
   time to time.
Maybe I'm just going through a
   phase.
I'll let you know next time I'm
   in town.
We both knew it couldn't last.
We've been going too fast. We
   both need a rest.
I'll call.
I want to be sure.
You're getting too serious.
I told you from the start I wasn't
   the sort to fall in love with.
I'm just not ready to commit.
No, of course it isn't anything
   you've done.
You're a wonderful person,
   but you're not the one for
   me.

You're too good for me.
We're too much alike.
We come from two different
   worlds.
It would break my mother's
   heart.
You're better off without me.
You'll get over me in time.
I'm doing this for your own
   good.
You'll thank me someday.
Let's be adults about this.
I know you wouldn't want to
   live a lie.
Sometimes people who really
   love each other have to
   separate.
I know how much you value
   honesty.
A clean break.
I thought he'd been killed in the
   war . . .
It's not my fault.
I'm trying to be fair.
I'm trying to be reasonable.
You have no one but yourself to
   blame.

**Adam and Amanda have been married for fifteen years. For
fifteen years she has cleaned the house, looked after the kids,
picked up his laundry, run his errands, listened to his tales of
corporate woe, ironed his clothes so that no one would ever
guess he didn't send them away to a French tailor, organized
and cooked for dinner parties that have made him the envy of
all the other executives in his firm, and become expert not
only at international law (his field) but at fly fishing (his**

hobby). One day, though, Adam looks in the mirror and notices those first grey hairs, those first patches of no hair, those crinkly little lines around his eyes that weren't there before. Adam sighs. He looks across the breakfast table at Amanda and notices that she has a few grey hairs and crinkles of her own. He falls in love with his new secretary. He asks Amanda for a divorce. 'But why, Adam?' sobs Amanda. 'Have I let you down? Have I been a bad wife? A poor mother? Can she make a better salmon mousse with avocado dressing than I can? Why do you want to leave me?' Adam says

Because being married to me has made you boring.

Reasons for not leaving your lover, even after you've been asked to go

I can't find a place of my own.
For the sake of the children.
I know you'll change your mind.
I can change, I swear it.
I'll never do it again.
One more chance.
One more try.
We can work this out.
I just don't understand why you can't forgive me.
I wouldn't want to see you do something you'll regret.
I know you don't really mean this.
It must be your time of the month.

The great blind-date lie

You might meet someone really wonderful.

What people tell you when they have someone totally unsuitable for you to go out with

I just know you two are really going to hit it off.
This isn't going to be like the last time.
He's not like other taxidermists. Just wait and see.

Trust me.
Who knows you better than I do?
Have I ever led you astray?
You think I'd set you up with someone you wouldn't like?
How do you ever expect to meet anyone if you don't go out?
You might be pleasantly surprised.
Wait till you see him.
My instincts are never wrong.
You're going to thank me.

Lies from the personal ads

Quiet good looks.
I'm not the sort of person who
    puts an ad in the personals.
Pleasant surprises await.
You won't be sorry.
I look like I should be taller.
Fun is my middle name.
Looks don't matter.

**You are out on your first date with this person who seems
pretty wonderful. Or at least better than average. Good
enough, at any rate, to deserve a second and maybe even a
third date. You certainly don't want to do anything to
discourage this person. That is why when this person launches
into a very long explanation of the sewage system in Venice
you don't interrupt for forty-five minutes and then what you
say is**

Wow, that's really fascinating.
I've always been very interested in plumbing.

**It is also why, when this person insists on ordering the
speciality in Tony's Tavern for the two of you – a speciality
that turns out to be spaghetti bolognese – instead of saying,
'I really hate spaghetti bolognese', which you do, you say**

Hm, this is delicious.

The great wedding lie

I will.

The first great male chauvinist lie

Penis envy.

The second

Nymphomania.

The lie a man will tell about a woman who isn't interested in him

She's frigid.

Another

Women don't know what they want.

Another

She must be a lesbian.

The last great male lie about sex

A man can always tell.

The last great lover's lie

Oh, darling, you shouldn't.

4
Let the Buyer Beware

Anyone who has ever bought a pair of shoes, had a telephone installed, or paid a small fortune to have the kitchen converted, knows that the person who coined the phrase 'Let the Buyer Beware' knew what she was talking about. Perhaps she'd been doing some comparison shopping for a refrigerator and had been puzzled by the lack of information your average salesperson likes to release. Or perhaps she'd been waiting seven weeks for the sofa to be delivered, only to discover when they finally decided to deliver it at a time when she was home, that they'd brought the wrong one. Perhaps she'd been forced to call a plumber. Who knows? Suffice to say that upon venturing into the outside world a person becomes aware quite quickly that though honesty may be the best policy it is not the one that most people use – especially when they're trying to sell you something, when they're trying not to deliver something, or when they don't feel really enthusiastic about repairing the roof. Look at it this way: if lies were snowfall, the lies of the market-place would be winter in Alaska and the lies between family, lovers and friends would be no more than a few random flakes that quickly turn to rain.

The first lie of the market-place

No one's asking you to buy anything.

The next ten

A real bargain.
Lowest prices in town.
Special offer.
Sale.
Massive reductions.
Money-back guarantee.
You won't be sorry.
Easy to assemble.
Easy to install.
One size fits all.

The next twenty-six

Free delivery.
Guaranteed Christmas delivery.
Safe, efficient and convenient.
There must be some mistake.
Your choice of colours.
Helpful, friendly sales clerks.

Just ask.
The customer is always right.
The customer always comes
   first.
We're here to serve you.
The experts.
Free estimate.
You won't know how you lived
   without it.
It won't run.
It won't fade.

One-hour service.
24-hour service.
We value your reactions.
It'll save you money.
Reliable.
Fully trained engineers.
Free loan set.
Once in a lifetime offer.
Easy finance.
You can't afford to be without it.
No waiting.

Great advertizing lies

New.
Innovative.
All new.
The best.
The whitest.
The cleanest.
The only.
Pure.
Just like mother used to make.
Luxury.
You won't know the difference.
You'll know the difference immediately.
Because you care.
Because we care.
You've never tasted anything like this before.
A new sensation.
Would we sell you something you didn't need?
Would we sell you something you didn't want?
A taste of paradise.
The real thing.
We want you to make up your own mind.
Long-lasting.
This book/washing-powder/ frozen pizza/microwave oven/fur coat
   will change your life.

You go into the local branch of a major nationwide chain of shops that sell electrical goods. You are interested in purchasing a portable cassette-player. Being a logical person, you go over to the section where these are sold. No one, such as a sales assistant, follows you. You walk up and down the aisles. You look at one portable cassette-player and then you look at another. Time passes. You look around for a sales assistant. You can see several in the distance. You stand up straight and put an expression on your face which is meant to convey the fact that you have not come into the shop because you wanted to get out of the rain but because you would like to use your credit card. Nothing happens. You wave hopefully at a sales assistant or two. They do not wave back. Finally you see a salesperson heading your way. As he draws near and you open your mouth to tell him what you want he says

I'll be right with you.

Several hours later, after you have finally found someone to serve you, you make your selection. The salesman informs you that that model, like the six previous ones you chose, is out of stock. A downcast look comes over your face. He then tells you three lies in quick succession

Two days.
I'll order it for you.
I'll ring you when it's in.

Other great salesmen's lies

May I help you?
It'll shrink.
It's so you.
It'll stretch.
Money well spent.
That is your size.
Of course.
A perfect fit.
I've got the same one at home.

It'll never give you any trouble.
That really suits you.
As it's you . . .
You never bought that here.
I can explain.
I'm trying to help you.
Our most popular model.
It's never been used.
I'm new here.

We're out of stock.
We'll replace it free of charge.
I'm having it sent over from our
    other shop.
Leave your name and number.

It was lost in transit.
I can't imagine how that
    happened.
Of course I'm sure.

Sometimes upstanding citizens lie to salespeople

I do take a ten.
I never took it out of the box.
It was like that when I bought it.
I followed the instructions to the letter.
It was nowhere near the heat.

What the young man in the paint shop told Marcia Clearwater when she ran out of paint on the last wall of the bedroom

We don't have a colour called yellow.

The great delivery lies

Monday.
Monday morning.
Monday afternoon.
The van broke down.
He rang the bell.
I can explain.
He rang the bell and phoned from the van.
There was no answer.
Our man has called three times.
He left it next door.
He left a card.
Tuesday for sure.
Of course it'll go up the stairs.
Of course it'll fit through the door.
It comes apart.
I don't do stairs.
I don't install.
Well they should have told you.
You have to specify.

The postman delivers a package during the only five minutes all week when you aren't in. He leaves a card to tell you that he has delivered a parcel when you weren't in. You tick the box that says you want the parcel redelivered and specify the day. The day comes and the day goes. You go to the post office and ask for your parcel. They don't have your parcel because they sent it back. You would like to know why they sent it back when you specifically asked to have the parcel redelivered. You would further like to know why they give you a card to fill out if they don't pay any attention to what it says. The postal clerk gives you the following explanation

Let's just say the card got lost in the post.

Great postal lies

Overnight delivery.
First class.
These things happen.
Do not bend.
Fragile.
Express.

We rarely lose anything.
It must have been incorrectly
    addressed.
It was a normal mistake.
Insured.

The reason the letter your cousin sent you in March arrives in June even though the postcode was correct

These things happen.

The reason your mother's Christmas present arrives at Easter

Christmas rush.

The lies repairmen tell you

Well, what time were you
    expecting me?
No one told me it was an
    emergency.
I can't see anything wrong.
That's why they call it an
    estimate.

It won't take long.
No job too big or too small.
I'll be right there.
I'll be there by noon.
Thursday afternoon for sure.
No later than eight-thirty.
I'll come back tomorrow.

I'll phone you next week.
I'm going to level with you.
Just a couple of days.
I'll have to shut off the water/
electricity for an hour.
No, only an hour.
That should do it.
I've never seen anything like
this before.
I'll just see if the part's come in.
Not too expensive.
Anybody else is going to tell you
the same thing.
I haven't got the tools with me.
Well, you could do it cheaper,
but you'd be sorry in the long
run.

I don't like the look of this.
You're not paying for my time,
you're paying for my
knowledge.
Of course it'll hold.
Look, if it were up to me . . .
Overheads.
I'll try to keep the costs down.
Minimum inconvenience.
Immediate, 24-hour emergency
service.
I'm only doing my job.
There's a good explanation.
Trust me.
I'll have to order the part.
About two days.

The lies repairmen tell you when they come back to fix either: a) what they were supposed to have fixed the first time; or b) what they broke when they fixed what they fixed the first time

I can't understand how that
happened.
Nothing like this has ever
happened before.
It has nothing to do with me.
It has nothing to do with the
first problem.
This happens all the time.

You must have touched it.
You must have dropped it.
I'll have to order the part.
Two days, maybe three.
Don't worry, it's under control
now.
Oh, now I see what went wrong.
This should do it this time.

The washing-machine, still under guarantee, starts pumping water into the kitchen instead of onto the clothes. You get out your service contract. It tells you that if something goes wrong you should not panic. You should call the number below. A repairman will be with you within twenty-four hours. He will repair on site. He will be fast, courteous and helpful. He is fully trained. Don't panic, says the contract, help is on

the way. You telephone. They say there will be someone with you tomorrow, but they can't say when. Could be in the morning. Could be in the afternoon. 'Couldn't you just give me an idea,' you beg. You laugh embarrassedly. 'I mean, I do have other things to do.' 'We can't commit to a time,' they say. You wait in all the next day. On the second day you phone again and ask what happened. 'Do you have a problem?' the voice on the other end of the phone wants to know. You explain your problem. 'An engineer will be with you tomorrow,' they promise. 'Look,' you say, 'I've already wasted one day on--' 'Madam,' they say, 'we are doing the best we can.' The engineer arrives the following afternoon at four-fifteen. He diagnoses the fault within ten minutes. 'No sweat,' says the engineer. 'So you can fix it,' you say. 'Sure,' says the engineer. 'I just have to order the part.' 'The part?' 'It'll come in a day or two. I'll be back.' Four days later, you telephone again to find out what terrible thing has happened to the engineer. 'Do you have a problem?' asks the voice on the other end of the line. You explain your problem. 'We'll send an engineer tomorrow.' 'But the engineer already came,' you say, your own voice a little whiney. 'Where do you live?' 'Look,' you begin, 'the man already ordered the part.' 'I'll just see if the part's come in.' Good news. The part has come in. The engineer will be with you the day after tomorrow, though they can't tell you precisely when. On the day after tomorrow, nine o'clock sharp, the engineer appears on the doorstep. Your heart skips a beat. It is not the same engineer, but what the heck. You explain the problem and the diagnosis the other engineer made. 'Yeah,' says the engineer, 'that's what I'd say it was. I'll order the part.' 'Order the part?' Something funny happens to your eyes. 'Order the part?' you repeat. 'But you're meant to have the part with you.' The engineer finds this amusing. 'I don't have the part,' he says. 'But,' you say, 'but they told me it was in. They told me they were going to give it to you.' The engineer smiles in a way that suggests he has come upon hysterical types like yourself before in this job. He says

Well, maybe it was the part they gave me yesterday. But it was broken.

What you tell the repairman when he wants to know who oiled the typewriter, was fooling around with the set, or tried to fix the stereo

No one.
Not me.
My friend from next door.
This guy I know.
One of the kids.
It was like that.
I don't know what you're talking about.

Other lies you tell the repairman

I don't know how it happened.
Just a couple of days.
It didn't seem serious.
It was like that when I got it.
I could still make out the picture.
Sometimes it worked if you jumped up and down.
I can't imagine how that got in there.

The reason it took three months to call a plumber to fix the hot-water tap in the kitchen

I kept forgetting.

The lie three separate electricians told Marcia Clearwater during the eighteen months that she tried to have the hall light repaired

I'll be back Wednesday.

What the man at head office told Marcia Clearwater one hour before the repairman turned up at her door

He can't come till next week.
I'm really sorry.

Builders' lies

I know exactly what you want.

It's not in my contract.

I never said Monday.

Under a thousand, I'm going to be honest with you.

That was last year.

You don't think I'm making any money on this job, do you?

There shouldn't be much dust.

There shouldn't be much noise.

It won't be for more than a day or two.

No problem.

We'll work around you.

You won't know we're here.

I'm only doing my job.

It's hard to say.

I'll let you know.

Soon.

Unforeseeable costs/delays/complications.

Don't worry about a thing.

You never said you wanted it finished off.

I know it's taking a little longer than we expected, but it'll be worth it in the end.

We're sorry for any inconvenience.

Satisfaction guaranteed.

Whatever you want.

Leave it to me.

I thought you wanted to keep the costs down.

We're done.

I wouldn't do this for everyone . . .

You come home from work to find the builder just finishing off in the kitchen. You are surprised to discover that, despite the several hours the two of you have spent poring over the blue-prints together and the reassurance he has given you over and over that he understood exactly what you wanted, he has put the cupboards where the stove was supposed to go. You express your puzzlement to him. He says

You wanted them on the other wall? Well, why didn't you say so?

The lie the builder told Marcia Clearwater every week for seven months when she wanted to know when he'd be finished

Friday, definitely.

Hysterical friends have warned you that in the process of stopping the rising damp from rising, a lot of dust will be generated. You ask the contractor if this is true. He says

No, there shouldn't be too much.
I wouldn't worry about it if I were you.

It took six nerve-wracking months for the builder to mend the leak in the roof. It got to the point where, if you heard someone say 'That should do it' one more time, you were going to strangle him. But at last all was well and dry. It rained and water didn't come pouring down on the couch. Whew!, you thought, this is great. Then it rained again. When you called the builder said

It can't have anything to do with the first problem.

The lies you tell the builder

It has nothing to do with money.
Nobody's blaming you.
Of course I understand.
My brother's a lawyer.

Car mechanics' lies

This afternoon.
Come back tomorrow.
Come back at five.
It's the battery.
Well, I can't imagine how that happened.
Of course I checked it.
You should have been able to drive it without the clutch.
I'll try to keep it reasonable.

You know what it's like with these old cars.
You'd be lucky to sell it for scrap.
I knew you wouldn't want to take the risk.
You won't have any more trouble with that.
Sure I'm sure.
Believe me.

Lies you tell your mechanic

I did have it changed.
I always check the oil.
I just put air in the tyres.
I did exactly what you told me.
It wasn't my fault.
All of a sudden it just came off in my hand.

You explained to your mechanic that you had to have the car by Friday because you're taking the family on your first holiday in three years on Friday. You've made your reservations, the ferry's been booked, and the builders are starting on the extension on Friday morning, making the house inhabitable for the next seven days, maybe eight. On Friday morning, your family staggering behind you with the luggage, you go to collect the car. The mechanic says

You wanted it today? Well, why didn't you say?

The lie the mechanic told Marcia Clearwater when he lost her ignition key

Nothing like this has ever happened before.

The reason why there is never any petrol left in your car when you collect it from the garage no matter how full the tank was to begin with

Test drive.

Buying-a-used-car lies

Perfect condition.
Needs some work.
Only 23,000 miles.
One owner.

Very reliable.
I'll fix it before you take it.
Leaving the country. Must sell.
A steal.

Buying anything used lies

I've never had any trouble with it.
Practically new.
As long as it goes to a good home . . .
It's too big for us.
It's too small for us.
It's just right for us, but someone gave us a new one.
There's been a lot of interest.
You're not the only one, you know.
I've had a better offer.
I can't tell you how much we hate to part with it.
It's like giving up part of my family.
I'll throw in the cups for nothing.
I had it all done by a professional.
Secondhand.
Because it's you.
Hardly worn.
Used once.
Unwanted gift.
Collector's item.

Painters' lies

If we say we'll be there, we'll be there.
You have to give it time to dry.
Of course that's Tangerine Tango.
Dark?
That was the estimate.
Two days at the most.
Monday for certain.
It's got nothing to do with the paint, it's your walls.
You're really going to like this.
I know what you want.
As a special favour to you . . .

Estate agents' lies

Three bedrooms.
Near the shops.
Economical to heat.
Quiet residential neighbourhood.
Spacious cupboards.
Room for another bath.
Perfect for a couple starting out.
Perfect for a growing family.
It would be easy enough to convert the spare room into another bathroom.
Sunny.
Needs some work.
The area is moving up.

I think we can get them to come down.
Convenient for public transport.
You won't get a bargain like this again.
Leave it to me.
Enormous potential.
There are several other parties interested.
DIYers' dream.
You won't even know it's there.
Old-world charm.
Exclusive neighbourhood.
No hidden costs.

Great movers' lies

Nine o'clock sharp.
Handle with care.
Expert packing.
We treat your belongings as our own.
Fast, efficient and reliable.
You never said anything about a piano.
Satisfaction guaranteed.

We don't do stairs.
These things happen.
You gave us the wrong directions.
That's the address you gave us.
Nothing like this has ever happened before.
That's not what I'm paid for.

Landlords' lies

I'll send the repairman around.
Fully furnished.
I'll take care of it.
Part of our agreement.
I don't know how you can accuse me of such a thing.
I'll be round on Monday.
I want to be fair.
I'm a reasonable man.
You mean they didn't come to fix the roof?
Trust me.

Lies of the launderette

Service wash.
All six machines broke at once.
You must have overloaded the machine.
That happens to be my machine.
That happens to be my sock.
I thought you were finished with the dryer.
You put in too much soap.
It'll be ready in an hour.
It was like that.
Hot water.
Change given.

You've received an electricity bill for £100 for a period when you hadn't yet moved into your home. You telephone the number that has been helpfully printed on the front of your bill and explain the situation to the young woman at the other end of the phone. She says

This is the wrong department. Wait a minute and I'll get you the number.

Five minutes later she comes back with the number you should have phoned in the first place. You explain your problem to the young man who answers. He says

Just hold on a minute.

Fifteen minutes later he gets back on the line. He says

Our records show an outstanding bill for £100.
I'm afraid it's not impossible.
Our computer does not make mistakes.

Bankers' lies

Insufficient funds.
We'd like to help you . . .
That isn't your signature.
We have no record . . .
Small service charge.
Three days.
We're here to help you.

We can't do that.
Just ask.
Someone will be with you in a
    minute.
It must have been lost in the
    post.

The great police lie

We'll send a man right around.

A few other great police lies

We'll get right on it.
There's nothing we can do.
We've done everything we can.

Internal investigation.
We police ourselves.

Lies people tell their babysitters

We won't be long.
He always sleeps right through.
She's never been any trouble
   before.
Did we forget to tell you about
   the light?
Just be firm and he'll go right
   back to sleep.
He's usually so well behaved.
She *cried*? I can't believe it. Did
   you hear that, darling, she
   cried for six hours straight.

Lies people tell their cleaners

You won't have to move
   anything heavy.
I'm not going to interfere.
I'd do it myself but I've got a
   bad back.
I don't want you to think I'm
   obsessive or anything . . .
I'll pay you on Friday.

Fashion lies

The new look.
Everybody's wearing it.
It makes you look thinner.
Youthful.
It makes you look taller.
It makes you look shorter.
It makes you look bustier.
Form flattering.
For the mature figure.
Exclusive.
Original design.

Hairdressers' lies

It's you. It's definitely you.
I know, I know, only a trim.
I'm not going to take too much off this time.
Trust me.
Of course the roots won't show.
No one else has ever complained.
I can just squeeze you in.

I can make you look just like Cher.
Your mother wouldn't be able to tell.
Come in and talk to one of our technicians.
You're paying for our expertise.
It's worth every penny.
You won't regret this.
Don't worry, I know exactly what you want.

Great newspaper lies

We have a responsibility to our
  readers.
A reliable source.
Exclusive.
You read it here first.
Impartial coverage.

Objective reporting.
Fearless reporting.
The true story.
Never before revealed.
The facts.
Unbiased.

Terms that reviewers use interchangeably and rather indiscriminately when they know the artist, know friends of the artist, have read everyone else's rave reviews, or can't think of anything else to say

A remarkable debut.
A brilliant debut.
An impressive debut.
Hilarious.
Unputdownable.
Brilliant.
A must.
Made me laugh out loud.
Beautifully written.

Moving.
A natural writer.
A born actor.
Best book of the year.
Best film of the year.
Best album of the year.
A masterpiece.
Magic.
A classic of its kind.

The phrase used to describe at least half a dozen singer-songwriters in the past ten years
The new Bruce Springsteen.

The phrase used to describe at least half a dozen singer-songwriters (including Bruce Springsteen) in the past twenty years

The new Bob Dylan.

The phrase used to describe at least a dozen different bands from the Rolling Stones to U2, including Bruce Springsteen and the E Street Band

The greatest rock and roll band in the world.

What people say when they either don't understand or fall asleep in the middle of a film, play, book, etc.

Interesting. Very very interesting.
Seminal.
Very deep.
Innovative.

Fascinating use of language/light/special effects.
Sensitive use of language/light/special effects.
Dazzling.

Memorable.
Moody.
Introspective.
Atmospheric.
Thought-provoking.
Very poignant portrayal.
Existential.
Haunting.
Oh, no I did like it.

Extraordinarily important for anyone who wants to truly appreciate the Czech cinema of the last forty years.
Reminiscent of Proust/Dickens/Faulkner/Melville/Salinger.
I have to think about it some more.

Great culture lies

No, but I saw the movie.
No, but I read the book.
No, but I've been meaning to.
There's nothing quite like the opera, is there?
I'm reading *Finnegan's Wake*.
No, for pleasure.
I've seen *Caravaggio* three times.
That's not quite as many times as I've seen *Women in Love*.
What? You mean you never saw Olivier on stage?
I never watch television.
I have the set for the kids.
I have the set for the occasional documentary on working
    conditions in Latin America or the life of the tree toad.
Everyone wants their children to learn to play the piano.
Violin music is so soothing.
Don't you feel that after *War and Peace* contemporary novels
    seem so *small*?
I always wished I'd been born during the Renaissance/Age of
    Reason/Golden Age of Rome.

**You have had a relatively pleasant meal in a local restaurant.
It's true the crisp salad had seen better days, and they'd run
out of your choice of dressings, and your idea of medium and
the chef's idea of medium are not quite the same, and the
helpful, courteous waitress practically threw your drink at
you just because you asked if she'd had to go far to get it, but
on the whole it wasn't bad. For dessert you order a banana**

split. As you delve into its depths you discover that for some reason it has come without anything that looks even faintly like a banana. You call the waitress over. She says

Oh, I'm so sorry. You must have been given someone else's sundae.
I can't imagine how that happened.
The ice cream chef is new.

Other untruths told by waitresses, waiters and menus

I'll be right with you.
It won't be a minute.
Your dinner's just coming.
Weren't you the garlic prawns?
Look, I wrote it down. Garlic prawns. Not fried chicken.
I hope you enjoy your meal.
Of course it's fresh.
We have to cook it specially.
A secret recipe.

No, I didn't forget your garlic bread.
This isn't my table.
I'm going as fast as I can.
Mixed salad.
A tantalizing blend . . .
Large.
Just ask.
Not too hot.
Service included.

Bureaucratic lies

I had it here a minute ago.
Not according to our records.
I'm afraid that's not handled by this office.
Mr _____ will be right with you.
It went out yesterday.
You can't do that over the telephone.
You'll have to telephone first.
We realize that it isn't your fault, nonetheless . . .
I'm afraid we are not responsible . . .
An unfortunate oversight.
An unfortunate computer error.
These things happen.
I hope you haven't been waiting long.
You've filled out the form incorrectly. You'll have to go back and start again.
You shouldn't have filled in this form. You should have filled in the other form.

Doctors' lies

You won't feel a thing.
There's nothing wrong.
The doctor will be right with
    you.
House calls.
I think I know what's best for
    you.
It should clear up in a day or
    two.
That's impossible.

Simple treatment.
Miracle drug.
No cause for concern.
Of course there aren't any side
    effects.
Perfectly harmless.
I'm sure it has nothing to do
    with the medication.
It's a very simple procedure.
The doctor knows best.

Solicitors' lies

I'm here to help you.
You have nothing to worry about.
I'll get back to you in a day or two.
Everything's under control.
We'll be in touch.
The other solicitor is being difficult.
I'm only human.
It's not going to be too expensive.
There have been a few additional expenses.
Yes, Mr _____, I see that makes sense. But I'm afraid it's a
    little more complicated than that.
I explained this fully at our first interview.
Trust me.
I have your best interests at heart.
I'm afraid the law doesn't really work that way.
Let justice be done.
I'll get right on it.

Great political lies

I have nothing to hide.
I challenge the press to follow me and see.
I know nothing about it.
I knew nothing about it.
I knew a little about it.

No comment.

It's only a rumour.

There's no truth in it at all.

There may have been a little more to it than I was aware of at the time.

I'll prove my innocence.

I never saw this woman/that man/that gun-runner before in my life.

I'm not prejudiced, but . . .

I'm not a racist, but . . .

I was only doing my job.

I had the best interests of this great nation at heart.

There is no conspiracy.

More great political lies

Public interest.

Safe levels.

No cause for concern.

Germany wants peace.

Russia wants peace.

America wants peace.

Peace in our time.

Military action [as in 'We're not at war, it's just a military action'].

Military advisers.

It'll be over by Christmas.

Everything that could possibly be done is being done.

You can trust us.

We all want to see this thing settled.

Everyone wants an equitable solution.

Cooperation.

No threat to local residents.

It's a matter of principle.

We're doing the best we can.

What Gerald Ford said upon landing in Yugoslavia after visiting the Soviet Union

It's nice to be out of the Communist Bloc.

One of the best

It became necessary to destroy the town to save it [US Army Major referring to Ben Tre, Vietnam, in 1968].

Another

I don't think it will come in my lifetime [Margaret Thatcher on the probability of there being a woman Prime Minister].

Further political lies

A conspiracy of Communists and Jewish bankers.
Better dead than red.
Poverty is a thing of the past.
Everything we do is for the good of everyone.
Freedom for all.

5
Personal Lies

You would think, wouldn't you, that the one place a person would be safe from all forms of dishonesty, deception and deceit would be in his or her own company. After all, how can you lie to someone who already knows everything about you that there is to know? Why lie to someone from whom you don't want anything, someone who has no choice but to like you, someone it is unnecessary to impress? You know that wasn't sunlight that lightened your hair. You know who ate the rest of the chocolate cake. You know you're not going to little Emily's piano recital come hell or high water, no matter what you may say to little Emily's parents. You certainly know that when you say, 'This is the year I get into shape,' there are no serious implications in that statement, no threat to your flabby muscles or your craving for chocolate; that, in fact, you have no intention of doing much more than buying a track suit, a rowing-machine, and a set of those little weights you can wiggle in the air while you're watching television. That when you say, 'I really wish I knew how to repair my own car,' getting your hands dirty and spending hours of video time learning the difference between the distributor drive gear and the camshaft drive gear are not what you have in mind.

And yet we are all so good at self-deceit you would be forgiven for assuming that it must be genetically coded. 'I'm not going to see Joe ever again,' you tell yourself. 'But I have to drop by once just to make sure he understands that I'm never going to see him again.' 'I'm going to open the bag of crisps,' you say to yourself, 'but I'm only going to eat one. Really.' No one ever understands why others accuse them of being selfish or stubborn, ungenerous or over-critical, manipulative or humourless. 'I'm not like that,' you say to yourself. 'Am I?' And your self replies, 'Not at all.'

One of the most striking differences between a giraffe and a human being is that a giraffe will never kid itself into thinking that it's going to clean out the loft on Saturday as it's been promising to do on every Saturday for the past twenty-three months, but a person will. The giraffe will say to itself, 'Hey, man, there is no way I'm cleaning out the loft when I could be out shopping, running up the balance due on my credit card and stopping in fast-food chains for onion rings and chips.' But the person will say, 'I'm going to get the loft done today, but first I'll just run into town to get some rubbish bags. I won't be a minute,' and comes back, six hours later, deeper in debt and with two day's caloric intake taken care of, and much too tired from lugging all those carrier-bags around all day to face the loft. As our person sinks into his armchair with a cup of tea, he says to himself, 'Next week I'm definitely going to do the loft. This time I really mean it.'

Bad habit lies

I can stop whenever I want.
Tomorrow.
I know I shouldn't, but . . .
It's no big deal.
I deserve it.
I'm impossible to live without my daily litre of cola.
Just this once.
Just one more.
It's not going to hurt me just to have one.
Today's the day I stop.

Really.
Definitely.
It's not as if it's every day.
It's not as if it's excessive.
It's not as if I'm doing anybody any harm.
This time I mean it.
I deserve it.
A person has to have a few pleasures in life.
What's life without chocolate?

Why you go into the garbage to retrieve the cigarettes/chocolates/bottle of tequila you threw away last night in a moment of resolution and strength

It's too good to waste.
I'll never do it again.

You have absolutely, positively forbidden yourself from entering any record shop – secondhand shops and W H Smith's included – for the next year. And yet here you are, standing outside one of the largest branches of one of the largest chains, your hand on the door. 'I'll just go in for five minutes,' you tell yourself, 'while I'm waiting for Farquah to turn up.' In you go. The entire multi-level store is throbbing to one of your favourite old songs. 'I'm not going to buy anything,' you say determinedly, your hand sliding into your wallet to feel the hardness of the credit card within. 'Nothing.' You look around at the rows and rows of timeless recordings, the new releases, the sales tables piled high with albums you'd always wished you owned. 'Maybe one thing that's on sale,' you amend. 'There's nothing wrong in that.' You finally reach the checkout twenty-three minutes later and heave the stack of LPs and tapes you've collected onto the counter. The young bald man at the till raises one eyebrow. 'You've just inherited?' he asks. With feverish conviction you say to the young bald man

I'm never going to buy another record as long as I live.

General reasons for not doing what you're supposed to do

I can do it later.	I'd better take a nap first.
I'm not in the mood.	It's too late.
Too many interruptions.	It's too early.
Too much noise.	It's too cold.
I really should re-pot the plants/	It's too sunny.
paint the flat/re-tile the	It's too damp.
kitchen before I do anything	I'll just make one phone call . . .
else.	

You promised to visit your old Granny who lives forty-five miles away, who doesn't get around much any more, who sees few people other than the health worker, the meals-on-wheels person and the milkman, and who never talks about anything that happened after 1929. But come the hour of your visit and you discover that you'd much rather fix yourself a snack and

watch that great movie on the television than drive through a
cold, dark and rainy night to hear about the argument Granny
had with her sister over a white dress in 1920. Here are the
reasons you don't do what you're supposed to do

It's raining.

You really don't feel all that well.

You've had a hard day.

You've had a rotten week.

It'll be late by the time you get there and Granny won't be up to
much anyway.

Granny will understand.

She goes to bed early anyway. You'll barely get there, then you'll
have to come back.

It makes more sense to go in the daytime, when you can stay
longer.

You shouldn't drive that far before you've checked the oil, and Lord
knows you're not checking the oil in the dark.

If you go another day, maybe Saturday if you don't clean out the
loft, or Sunday if you're not too busy, you'll not only be able to
spend more time, but you might even be able to take Granny for
a drive or out for lunch, and wouldn't she just love that?

Yes, she would definitely love that. It would be much better than
popping in for a quick visit when she's tired and you're tired and
you have to get up early for work. You'll visit Saturday. Or
Sunday. Unless something comes up.

**Despite the fact that if she makes one more purchase with her
credit card her bank manager is going to burst through the
doors of the shop and vault over the checkout screaming, 'Put
that down, Ms Clearwater! We don't need another paisley
bandana!', Marcia Clearwater often finds herself entering the
shopping centre when she should be at home cleaning the
oven. Here's how she explains this to herself**

I need some new oven cleaner anyway.

I'm not going to buy anything, I'm just going to look.

I've been depressed. It'll cheer me up.

I deserve a treat.

It's almost Christmas/my birthday/Chinese New Year.

I don't have anything in that shade of blue.
It's in the sale.
They're practically giving it away.
At this price, I can't afford not to buy it.
They may not have it in stock for much longer.
Actually, I really need it.
It's not as if I spend a lot of money on other things.
I'll never buy anything again as long as I live.
Never.

Reasons for not checking the oil, the tyre pressure, or the brake fluid

It's raining.
It's too dark.
I'm not in the right mood.
I'm too tired.
How about that, I forgot again!
I'll do it tomorrow.
Nothing's going to happen if I leave it one more day.

It'll be all right for one more day.
No one else ever bothers, what am I worried about?
These things are built for neglect.

Reasons for never answering letters

I meant to.
I'm going to.
Tomorrow.
At the weekend.
I've been so busy, I just never have a chance.
I can't find a pen.
I can't find any paper.
I don't have any stamps.
They won't answer.
No one ever writes to me.
I have to be in the mood.
I started a letter.
I started a letter but I can't find it.
I started a letter but now it's all out of date so I'll have to start it again.

Reasons for never beginning that evening class

I missed the registration day.
I was ill the first week.
It's been raining so much.
Next term definitely.
By the time I get home from work I'm so tired . . .
I can't get anyone to look after the kids.
The class I wanted was full.
The course I wanted is too far away.
Mondays are impossible.
I had all that trouble with my elbow.

Reasons for never going to that evening class once you've registered

I'm really too tired tonight.
They're all more advanced than I am.
I don't like the instructor.
The instructor doesn't like me.
It starts too late.
You have to be in the mood.
I've had this rotten cold.
The room isn't heated.
There's not much point in going if you've missed the first class.
I can't stand that little man who's always showing off.

Reasons for never starting your novel, your violin lessons, that stained glass window you've been meaning to make for the hall

I'm too busy.
I'm too tired.
Where am I supposed to do it? In the kitchen?
It's all there, in my head, I just have to set it down.
A person has to have a social life.
When am I supposed to do it? In my sleep?
As soon as I finish cleaning out the loft . . .
As soon as the weather clears up . . .
As soon as the kids leave home . . .
As soon as my brother goes back to Okinawa . . .
As soon as I get the money together for a word processor/new bow/ oven.
In the spring.
It's not my fault.

The reason the loft is never cleaned, the stereo is never fixed, the light is out in the kitchen for eleven months, the garden is never weeded, and there is a rectangle of cardboard in the upstairs window instead of a pane of glass

I'm going to do it.

What you say to anyone who asks that tricky question 'When?'

What would you like me to do, quit my job?

Looking-in-the-mirror lies

Not bad.
Pretty good.
I don't really look that old.
What a hat.
That cream really works.
You wouldn't even know I was wearing make-up.
It hides my stomach.

It hides my legs.
I've always looked very good in purple.
No one else will notice.
Maybe if I just wear something with a high neck . . .
I don't think this makes me look fat.
With long sleeves . . .
With a hood . . .
I just have to remember to stand straight.
There must be something wrong with this mirror.

The reason thousands of men grow twelve strands of hair six inches longer than the rest and comb them straight over the top of their heads

So no one will notice that they're going bald.

Why people wear contacts that irritate their eyes and fall out in crowded stores so that everyone has to freeze in place until they're found

So no one will know that they need glasses.

The standing-on-the-scales lies

It must be broken.
Water retention.
My socks must weigh at least a pound.
You always weigh more in the morning.
You always weigh more at night.

The first fantastic diet lie

This time I'm really going to stick to it.
No, really.

The second

It's not fattening.

The third

I'll just have one.

The fourth

But I didn't eat anything all day.

The fifth

It's my glands.

The sixth

It's my metabolism.

The seventh

It must have shrunk.

The eighth

It must be cut small.

The ninth

A diet's fine, but I have to keep up my strength.

The tenth

I'll just have one.

The eleventh

You've got to eat *something*.

The twelfth

Feed a cold.

The thirteenth

I don't really care for sweets.

The fourteenth

Two's my limit.

Those other dieting lies

Lose weight without dieting.
Lose weight without trying.
Burn up calories.
Tastes just like chocolate/white lasagne/chicken satay with peanut sauce but at half the calories.
You won't know the difference.
Lose ten pounds in three days.
Takes it off and keeps it off.
The diet that's worked for millions.
Never feel hungry again.
Non-addictive.
Three days to a new, slimmer you!
You can never be too thin.

The twelve great diet lies you tell yourself while standing in front of the fridge with the door open at four in the afternoon on a rainy Sunday

I won't eat anything else for the rest of the day.
I'm feeling a little faint.
I didn't put any milk in my tea, so I can have one biscuit.
I'll just take a taste.
Cheese is good for you.
Nobody eats celery just on its own.
An apple, a handful of raisins and a few carrots don't count.
If I don't eat I'll get a headache.
I'll never be able to clean out the loft without some energy.
I'll have my lips sewn together in the morning.
You can't diet for ever.

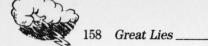

Marcia Clearwater's great diet lies when confronted by an empty custard creams packet

Who ate all the biscuits?
I only had one or two.
I don't remember.
Well, it certainly wasn't me.
I don't even like custard creams.
I threw them away.

'What's that?' asks your best friend, pointing to the empty custard creams packet on the sofa. 'An empty custard creams packet,' you say honestly, brushing the last stray crumbs from your lips. 'But I thought you were on a diet,' says your friend.

I am.

Your friend eyes you quizzically

But not today.

The quizzical eyeing continues

I'm starting tomorrow.

The gimlet gaze doesn't falter

For heaven's sake, no one diets on the weekend.

Marcia Clearwater's all-time prize-winning diet lie when confronted in the morning with biscuit crumbs on the kitchen table and a knife covered with peanut butter and jelly in the sink

I must have been asleep.

Vanity lies

I'm too handsome for my own good.
They can't keep their hands off me.
Everybody says I should have been a model.
If I wasn't so nice I wouldn't have all these problems.
I shouldn't be so selfless.
Other people aren't as generous as I am.
No one else works as hard as I do.
I was wrong once. I thought I was wrong about something and I
    wasn't.
I don't know where they'd all be if it weren't for me.
On me it looks good.
They're going to miss me.
I don't know what she's talking about, it doesn't make me look fat.
It's not too loud.
Look at the stuff Elton John gets away with . . .

**You're waiting for a bus with Marcia Clearwater. 'Here comes
one now!' you exclaim, pointing up the road where a large red
bus is trundling towards you. 'How can you tell?' asks Marcia.
'Because there's a bus at the next corner,' you say. You've
never taken LSD, so you know you can't be having one of
those acid flashbacks. 'Boy,' says Marcia. 'You must really
have good eyesight.' 'Marcia,' you say, 'do you need to wear
glasses?' Marcia says**

No.
Not really.

What you say when you don't get the job

I didn't really want it anyway.
They gave it to the boss's niece/girlfriend/daughter/cousin.
I was over-qualified.
They only advertised because they had to. They always knew who
    they were going to give it to.
I applied too late.
I only applied for the heck of it.

I knew I wasn't going to get it.
Something better's bound to come along.
I think they found me too threatening.
I probably would have hated it.

What you say when you don't win the contest

I applied too late.
   It's obvious they were looking for something more commercial.
It was probably rigged.
My entry must have gotten lost in the post.

6
Working Lies

The business of this planet is business. And all employers, of course, are upright, outstanding citizens who have nothing but the good of the world at heart and who do everything they can to ensure that their employees are treated with respect and dignity, and are given a good working environment and a fair wage. No employer in this day and age would ever do anything illegal, put the lives of employees at risk, cut corners in a dangerous manner, endanger the environment, or trade with the evil or the insane just to make a profit.

And, likewise, work is what separates man from the animals. Work gives us dignity. Work allows us to use our brains, imaginations and creativity in a useful and productive way. Work gives our lives meaning. People who don't work, unless they are royalty or have inherited fortunes or are involved in 'art', are no good, anti-social, anti-society, enemies of the State and part of the underserving poor. Additionally, of course, all good workers are honest and forthright, do the best job they know how, and follow their consciences rather than their paychecks.

And if you believe all of that, you'll believe all that follows.

Employers' lies

Full benefits package.
Competitive salaries.
Excellent working conditions.
What's good for the business is good for you.
Management is looking into it.
Of course we're always happy to talk.
Negotiable.
My door is always open.
We have our reasons.
Trust us.

A great employer fabrication

Our key aim was to find the best possible working environment for
our employees.

**What the company spokesman, standing on the shore-line that
had seen the worst pollution disaster in history (from which
it had not recovered), had to say**

I can't tell you how good it makes you feel to see this beach.

**What employers call the drinks machine, the snacks machine
and the crisp dispenser in that windowless room behind the
toilets**

The canteen.

**You work for a company that manufactures novelties. Every
year you receive a small animal made out of a painted rock, a
tuft of some carcinogenic man-made material and plastic eyes.
This is called your**

Christmas bonus.

**When all the things your employers have always promised you
will happen**

Next year.

**Every year your employer makes everyone go on the company
picnic, where you are entitled to two hamburgers, two cans of
beer and a packet of crisps. The highlight of the company
picnic is the football game between management and staff,
which staff has learned over the years not to win by too much.
This picnic is called**

Cementing good relations.
Having fun.

The reason you can't have a rise

You won't be motivated to increase production for the next six
    months.
Profits aren't up to predictions.
Inflation.
The company needs to reinvest.
We don't want to reduce your contribution to this company to mere
    money.

The reason you can't have a raise but the directors all have company cars, expense accounts, and annual conferences in the Bahamas

We have to cut unnecessary expenses.
It's harder at the top than it looks.

The reason the company does not have a crèche

If women want to have children it's their own business.

The reason all the really important jobs still go to men

Men are just better at some things. [This may not really be a lie, of
    course, because no one has ever actually made clear 'better than
    what'. Than three-toed sloths? Than visitors from Alpha Centuri?
    Than nothing?]

The great work myths

Job satisfaction.
Indispensable. [As in: 'I am indispensable to the smooth working of
    this company'; or 'Jones, you are indispensable to the smooth
    working of this company, so let's see you do another thirty-six
hours in overtime and we'll see about compensation later.']
We here at _____ are just one big happy family.
A fair day's work for a fair day's pay.
Free enterprise.
Our economy works on a system of supply and demand.
Industry does not exist solely to make a profit.

Lies between business partners

Leave it to me.
If you can't trust your own
   partner, who can you trust?
It's under control.
It was an honest mistake.

This sort of thing could happen
   to anyone.
It wasn't my fault.
Well, it certainly wasn't mine.

**You've been trying to have a talk with your boss about
something that is important to you but an annoying piece of
administration to him. Whenever you telephone, his secretary
says**

I'm sorry, he's busy right now.
He's in a meeting.
He just stepped out.

The great secretary lies

I'll have him phone you back.
She's not back yet.
He's been unavoidably detained.
She hopes you haven't been inconvenienced.
We're so sorry.

Other lies of the well-trained secretary

He just wrote you a letter.
I'm not sure what was in it.
She was just trying to get hold of you.
He asked me to give you his apologies.
I can't find her diary.
Yes, he understands it's urgent.
I'm afraid that her diary's full for the next two weeks.
I gave him your message.

You should have received it by now.
She was in a meeting all afternoon.
I'm sorry but he cannot be disturbed.
She'll be back in an hour.
He's at lunch.
She's on the other line.
I'll tell him you called.

Receptionists' lies

It's ringing.
I'm putting you through.
If you'll just hold for a minute.
I'm afraid there's no one here by that name.
Would you like to leave a message
I'll give her your message.
I gave him your message.

Lies agents tell their clients

I talked to _____ and everyone there is very excited.

I did it yesterday.

I was in a meeting.

I was in a meeting talking about you.

I was in a meeting in Australia talking about you.

There's nothing to worry about.

It's under control.

Trust me.

I love it. Absolutely love it.

I really let them have it, believe me.

My hands are tied.

You were the first person I thought of for this project.

Let me handle this, they'll listen to me.

No, I don't think you're being unreasonable.

What lunch?

I did call you back.

I never got your message.

I tried everything.

I do think they have a point. No, just a little point.

It must have been lost in the post.

There aren't going to be any problems.

You don't know how hard I work for you.

You think it's easy, what I do? The meetings, the lunches, the cocktail parties . . .

There's not going to be any problem getting backers . . .

Nothing's going to go wrong.

What Roman Polanski was told when he first suggested a film of Macbeth

Roman, baby, Shakespeare isn't big box office.

Lies clients tell their agents

It's almost finished.

By Monday.

I never answer the phone when I'm working.

I've been here all the time.

I'm not being unreasonable.

Of course I read the contract.

The director really liked the idea.

Nothing's going to go wrong.

The editor said she thought it was fine.

I know I impressed them.

You mean you haven't gotten it yet?
Of course I want your honest opinion.
I've been working day and night.
I know you work very hard for me . . .
I really think you're going to love this.
Oh, it's not very interesting . . .
Oh, you don't have to read it right now.

Publishers' lies

It's wonderful. Wonderful. I just have one or two little points.
You're the boss.
It's our standard contract.
No one's trying to pull a fast one on you.
If it was just me I wouldn't change a thing, but . . .
You know what these copy editors are like.
You know what these salesmen are like.
You know what these Americans [British/Japanese/Yugoslavians/
    Germans/Hebridean Islanders] are like.
I've been trying to get you all afternoon.
I was up all night working on your manuscript.
It must have got lost in the post.
It's a wonderful story, but it's not what we call commercial.
We're all on your side.
Of course we're sensitive to your needs.
You don't need to advertise a book like this. Word of mouth is what
    really matters.
You think publishers don't know how important authors are?
We did everything we could.
Didn't our publicity department call you?
You mean you haven't received your cheque yet?
What photographs?
It must have been an oversight.
I was hoping you'd call.
I'd love to, I'd really love to, but I've got a sales conference coming
    up.
We'll have to see what the budget looks like.
We'll have to wait for the reviews.
I'm sorry about lunch, but this meeting's just been called.
We sent the contract weeks ago.

What publishers say when authors call them up wanting to know why they can't find their books in the shops

It's not our fault.

Lies authors tell their publishers

Just one more week.
Nearly there.
I've been ill.
I had no idea there was really someone named Haycroft F. Wilson.
I welcome constructive criticism.
Of course you can be honest with me.
My agent never mentioned that.
You know what agents are like, ha ha ha.
You're not the only one who was interested, you know.
It's going very well.
I want it to be perfect.
Look, I'm not trying to be one of those nervous, nagging authors . . .

Working-person lies

I think I've got the 'flu.
I put it on your desk this
    morning.
I know we agreed that you
    would do it.
I'm sorry I'm late.
Who's been moving things on
    my desk?
What memo?
My wife has to go to the
    doctor . . .
It wasn't my fault.
Fergusson was going to do it.
I was in the loo.
I was just about to do it.
It's not a bad job.
I mean it this time. If they don't
    do something about_____
    I'm going to quit.

The great twentieth-century work lie

It's the unions that cause all the trouble.

The other three

I'm working.
I am working.
This is work.

7
Travel Lies

There used to be a time when you could be born in the village of Little Chipmunk and die in the village of Little Chipmunk, only leaving once, to go across the valley to Big Chipmunk for your second cousin's wedding. In those days, you never had to trust foreigners, strangers, bus conductors or travel agents for your safety, comfort, well-being, or actual arrival at your destination. Now that we are all part of the great global community, however, patrons of restaurants and snack bars that all look exactly the same and serve the same weak coffee and day-old sandwiches whether you're in Wapping or Tasmania, few people stay home for more than a day or two.

The first time you venture off the block all on your own, you can't help feeling a little nervous and apprehensive. What if I don't know what stop to get off at? you wonder. What if there's no one waiting to meet me from the train? How do I get from the airport to the hotel? Does everyone in Europe really speak English? 'Don't worry about a thing,' everyone reassures you. 'You'll be fine.' 'I will?' you ask. 'Sure. No problem. Not a thing to worry about.' Oh, right, you think to yourself, well that's good to know. The conductor will tell me when to get off the bus. The ticket collector will make sure I'm on the right train. The travel agent will arrange for transport to the hotel. Everyone in Europe not only speaks fluent English but they all like us a lot. It is as you look up from the book you brought along for the journey and notice a river you don't remember seeing before that it occurs to you that travel may not be so simple after all. It is as you get off the train whose destination was Liverpool and find everyone speaking with broad Scottish accents that you first realize that of all the things that travel, lies travel best of all. Whether you are taking the bus to Aunt Sophie's for a quick cup of tea (you can't stay long, you've got a million things to do), or are broadening your horizons by going to Majorca to see what the fish and chips there are like, travelling offers a person countless opportunities for expanding their repertoire of distortions of the truth.

The first great travel lie

The earth is flat.

The second

You're going to have a great time.

The third

Travel is a broadening experience.

The fourth

Getting there is half the fun.

The bus stopped; and then, without warning, the bus started again. In between, an elderly woman who had been waiting at the stop for the past seventy-eight minutes attempted to board the bus. Stooping to lift her out of the road, the conductor said

It's your own fault.
You could see we weren't stopped.
Never get on a moving vehicle.

Public transport lies

Regular service.
One every ten minutes.
Night bus.
We welcome your suggestions.
Fast and efficient.

We're doing everything we can
   to improve our service.
Travel in comfort.
Always on time.
Almost always on time.

Bus conductors' lies

Sure I'll tell you.
Yes, it's on our route.
We were held up in traffic.
There's another bus right behind us.

I don't have any change.
There's room upstairs.
It's against the regulations.
I didn't see you.
Full up.

Railway lies

Unforeseeable delay.
Service will be restored as soon as possible.
We're putting on extra trains.
It's the weather.
Yes, that's the train you want.
Buffet car.
Leaving on time.

Arriving on time.
No delays.
On schedule.
Obstruction on the track.
Your watch must be fast.
There was an announcement.
Thank you.

**Why, according to the management, no one can ever
understand the announcements made over the tannoy at
railway stations, bus depots and tube platforms**

Because they don't pay attention.

**You and several hundred other people have been waiting on
platform 2 for the southbound express for nearly an hour.
Suddenly there is an announcement. Heads are raised
expectantly. The sound coming from the tannoy seems to be
a message spoken in Greek and transmitted by a pirate radio
station off the coast of Alaska during a severe storm. When it
ends, half of the people on the platform head for the stairs.
You grab the person nearest you and say, 'Is that what the
message said? To leave the platform?' She says**

Yes.

**Because the bus that is meant to come every twelve and a half
minutes came only after you'd waited for forty minutes, you
arrive at the train station with seven minutes to spare before
the three fifty-five to Milton Keynes is due to leave. You
decide not to drive yourself crazy by standing in a ticket
queue and race over to one of the new, handy, convenient and
easy-to-use ticket machines. By the time you have worked out
the complicated ritual which will get you a ticket, you have
two minutes to get to platform 11. Oddly enough, when you
get to platform 11 you find a sign there that points towards
the ice cream stall and says Go To Platform 16. You slide into
the entrance to platform 16 as the clock overhead registers
three fifty-four – and as the train to Milton Keynes
disappears around a bend. 'But it's not supposed to leave for
another minute!' you shout at the railway employee standing
by the barrier. The railway employee says**

That clock's wrong.

Great taxi-driver lies

Yeah, I know where you mean.
Fifteen minutes.
No, it's not far.
I thought you said Heathrow.
It's a one-way system.
It's a short cut.

I know where I'm going.
There's nothing illegal about doing a U-turn on the motorway.
I've never had an accident in twenty years.

As the cab speeds off into the night, you lean forward and tap on the sheet of plastic that separates you from the driver. 'Excuse me,' you say. Although your voice is the only sound to be heard within the car, he doesn't hear you. You rap. 'Excuse me,' you scream. 'Excuse me!' His eyes meet yours in the rear-view mirror. 'I just wondered if you'd like to know that we're going in the wrong direction,' you say. He says, 'What?' You repeat yourself. He says

No we're not.

What they tell you when you order a cab

Ten minutes.
He's on his way.
He's outside now.
He should be there by now.
He rang the bell.
Are you sure you gave me the right address?
When did you order it?
I beeped the horn.

You explain to the person on the other end of the phone that he should tell the cab driver to wait a few minutes before he decides that he's got the wrong address because you're at the top of the building and it takes a while for you to get down the stairs. The person on the phone assures you that he understands. 'Yeah, right,' he says. 'Don't worry about it.' The minute you see the cab stop outside you race for the door. You take the stairs two at a time. You hit the front step just as the cab starts to pull away. You run after it, waving and screaming. When you call the cab company back to ask why the driver didn't give you enough time to get outside, the person on the phone says

He did.

The great directions lie

You can't get there from here.

Airport lies

Easy to get to.
Plenty of check-ins.
Plenty of parking.
Courteous, efficient staff.

Airline lies

High-quality service.
Comfortable seats.
Easy check-in.
Delicious meals.
You'll love our stewardesses.
Best fares.
Free drinks.
No cause for alarm.

You'll never know you've left
  the ground.
Slight turbulence.
A slight delay.
Every effort is being made . . .
We're sorry for the
  inconvenience.
French air-traffic controllers.

Why your luggage is in Nova Scotia but you are not

Just a little mix-up.

Why no one ever pays any attention when the attendants explain how to inflate the life preserver, use the little whistle, and make the tiny light go on so that the rescue planes will find you

They already know all about it.

The gentleman ahead of you is heaving along a small trunk as hand luggage. The young woman checking the boarding cards says to him, 'I'm sorry sir, but I think that is over your limit.' He, mopping the sweat from his brow, says

This?
Really?
Are you sure?

The reason they don't have your vegetarian meal

There must be some mistake.
You couldn't have ordered it.

Why there is water pouring in from the seam just above you

Condensation.

Why no one ever answers your calls for an attendant

It's not their station.

When you finally climb over six other passengers and fight your way to the attendants' cubby-hole to see if there's any chance of getting a glass of water or heating up the baby's bottle, the attendant, busy trying to get some coffee into a businessman who is not drunk, says

I'll be right with you.

Why you spend twelve hours scrunched into a plastic chair, waiting for your flight to depart

Unavoidable delays.

Travel agent lies

Bargain rates.
Luxury accommodation.
A view of the sea.
For the discriminating holidaymaker.
Our representative will meet you at the airport. [This is, of course, not necessarily a lie. Sometimes their representative does meet you at the airport. What they fail to mention, however, is that their representative rarely speaks your language.]
Of course you'll have time to make the connection.
Personally, I'd rather fly with them than one of the bigger airlines.
Your own bathroom, colour television and an amazing view.
Totally refurbished.
Exceptional value.
See the real Italy/France/Greece/Spain/Germany/Norway few tourists ever see.
A slight change in arrangements.
Thirteen months of sunshine.
It never rains at this time of year.
We didn't say there weren't any mosquitoes.

Great global lies

The French are great cooks.
The English are always
    gentlemen.
The Italians are great lovers.
The Americans are so friendly.
Gemutlichkeit.

Mother India.
Romantic Africa.
The exotic East.
You haven't lived till you've seen
    nightfall in Nairobi.

What the women standing next to you at Stonehenge had to say about the landscape

It's just like Wisconsin.

Hotel lies

Full bath.
Room service.
You didn't confirm your reservation.
Something may come up.
We'll page you if they phone.
When did you book your room?
It says here single.
The manager wishes me to tell you how sorry she is . . .

8
Universal
Lies

We talk a lot about universal truths. In spite of all the things that divide us, we maintain that there are certain things – such as language and custom, history and tradition, and the fact that you cannot get a decent blueberry pancake in England or a real English sausage in Tuscany or brown bread in Spain – that hold us together, that make us all part of one great human family. Universal truths. Which is not, of course, what we mean at all. What we mean are universal lies; those slight alterations of the truth that are passed down from generation to generation, those phrases of deceit that are so commonplace as to have become parts of standard thought and speech. Be you in Bangkok or Portsmouth, when the earnest-looking man in the white shirt and thinning hair leans across the counter and says to you, 'Come back in the morning,' you know without having to check in the dictionary exactly what he means. He means you're never going to get your passport back. Be you in Prague or San Francisco, when the guard slams the gate in your face and says, 'There'll be another one along in a minute,' you know it's time to look for a beach to crash on.

Universal lies – able to leap national boundaries in one bound.

The greatest universal lie

Your cheque is in the post.

Great all-purpose lies

No cause for concern.
It's really quite simple.
Just as a precaution.
Just for an hour or two.
Nothing like this has ever
  happened before.
Everything's under control.
It won't be long.

You won't notice the difference.
Circumstances beyond our
  control.
We're doing everything we can.
You can't lose.
Trust us.
Everybody does it.

The Albert Einstein lie

God doesn't play dice.

Other universal lies

The weaker sex.
Honesty is the best policy.
Good always triumphs over evil.

The pen is mightier than the
  sword.
Penis envy.

This time is going to be
   different.
Public service.
What you don't know can't hurt
   you.
Normal.

Average.
No one would be stupid enough
   to push the button.
Holy war.
Perfectly safe.
Unavoidably detained.

The greatest lies passed down through the ages

Man is separated from the animals by his superior intelligence.
Things can't get worse.
Absence makes the heart grow fonder.
Love conquers all.
All the world loves a lover.
The truth will out.
Christian brotherhood.
It's all for the best.
A natural mistake.

Three great reasons for anything

I had no choice . . .
It wasn't my idea . . .
It was just one of those things . . .

The penultimate great lie

No one's trying to destroy this planet.

The last great lie

Would I lie to you?